Stitch by Stitch

Volume 4

TORSTAR BOOKS

NEW YORK · TORONTO

Stitch by Stitch

TORSTAR BOOKS INC.
300 E.42ND STREET
NEW YORK, NY 10017

Knitting and crochet abbreviations

approx = approximately
beg = begin(ning)
ch = chain(s)·
cm = centimeter(s)
cont = continue(ing)
dc = double crochet
dec = decreas(e)(ing)
dtr = double triple
foll = follow(ing)
g = gram(s)
grp = group(s)
dc = half double
  crochet

in = inch(es)
inc = increas(e)(ing)
K = knit
oz = ounce(s)
P = purl
patt = pattern
psso = pass slipped
  stitch over
rem = remain(ing)
rep = repeat
RS = right side
sc = single crochet
sl = slip

sl st = slip stitch
sp = space(s)
st(s) = stitch(es)
tbl = through back of
  loop(s)
tog = together
tr = triple crochet
WS = wrong side
wyib = with yarn in
  back
wyif = with yarn in front
yd = yard(s)
yo = yarn over

A guide to the pattern sizes

		10	12	14	16	18	20
Bust	in	32½	34	36	38	40	42
	cm	83	87	92	97	102	107
Waist	in	25	26½	28	30	32	34
	cm	64	67	71	76	81	87
Hips	in	34½	36	38	40	42	44
	cm	88	92	97	102	107	112

Torstar Books also offers a range of acrylic book stands, designed to keep instructional books such as *Stitch by Stitch* open, flat and upright while leaving the hands free for practical work.

For information write to Torstar Books Inc., 300 E.42nd Street, New York, NY 10017.

Library of Congress Cataloging in Publication Data
Main entry under title:

Stitch by stitch.

  Includes index.
  1. Needlework. I. Torstar Books (Firm)
TT705.S74 1984   746.4   84-111
ISBN 0-920269-00-1 (set)

98765432

© Marshall Cavendish Limited 1984

Printed in Belgium

ISBN 0-920269-04-4   (Volume 4)

Contents

Crochet / COURSE 15

Working flat, circular motifs

Working circles in crochet is an important technique, since it is widely used to produce a variety of household items and fabrics.

The basic circle is made of a small number of stitches that are then increased evenly on each round until the motif is the size required. You can use any of a number of yarns — raffia and string, as well as fine crochet cotton — to achieve a variety of different effects with the same basic shape. In this course we show you how to work two of the simplest round motifs. Once you have mastered the basic technique, you can progress to a more complicated design.

1 Use knitting worsted and size G (4.50mm) hook for this sample. Make 5 chains and join them into a circle with a slip stitch.

2 Make 3 chains to count as the first double of the round. Now work 15 doubles into the center of the circle. You may have to push the stitches together to fit them all into the circle.

3 Join the last double to the 3rd of the first 3 chains with a slip stitch. There will now be 16 doubles in the circle, counting the first 3 chains as 1 double.

4 Make 3 chains. Now work 2 doubles into each stitch all the way around the circle. Complete the round by working 1 double into the stitch at the base of the first 3 chains, and join this to the top of these chains as before. There should be 32 doubles worked in the 2nd round.

5 Begin the 3rd round by working 3 chains as before. Now work 1 double into the next double and then 2 doubles into the next stitch on the previous round. The first increase has now been made.

6 Work around circle in the same way, working 2 doubles into every other stitch. Work last double into stitch at base of chain. Join last stitch to first 3 chains as before. There should be 48 doubles in the circle.

7 Work the next round in the same way, but work 2 doubles into every 3rd stitch instead of every other stitch as on the previous round.

8 Work the last double into the stitch at the base of the first 3 chains. Join with a slip stitch as before. There should now be 64 stitches in the circle.

Note Patterns for flat motifs are carefully devised to ensure that the motif lies flat. If you are adapting or designing a motif of your own, you will need to pay special attention to the number of increases you make on each round: with too few increased stitches, the motif will curl up at the edges and with too many increased stitches, the finished motif will have a fluted appearance.

9 Continue to increase 16 stitches on each round in the same way, working 1 more double between each increase on every subsequent round.

10 Work a total of 6 rounds for a motif approximately 6¼in (16cm) in diameter. There should be a total of 96 doubles worked in the last round.

An openwork motif

This openwork motif demonstrates the use of spaces to make a flat circular shape, using the spaces for increasing on each round. Try working the motif in a different kind of material, such as a thick cotton or string; or work each round in a different color to vary the completed motif.

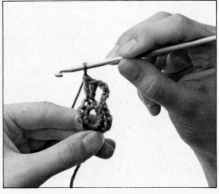

1 Make 6 chains and join them to form a ring with a slip stitch. Make 1 chain and then work 12 single crochets into the center of the ring. You may have to push the stitches together while working in order to fit them into the circle.

2 Make 5 chains to count as the first double and 2 chain space of the 2nd round. Skip the next stitch of the previous round and work 2 doubles into the next stitch.

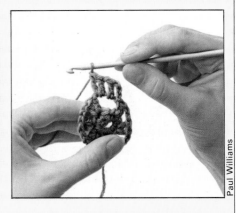

3 Work 2 chains. Skip the next stitch and work 2 doubles into the following stitch. Repeat this step 3 times more.

4 Now work 2 chains and then 1 double into the stitch at the base of the first 5 chains to complete the round. Join the last stitch to the 3rd of the first 5 chains with a slip stitch. There should be 6 groups of doubles in all.

5 Begin the 3rd round with 3 chains. Now work 1 double followed by 1 chain and then 2 doubles all into the first space in previous round.

Paul Williams

continued

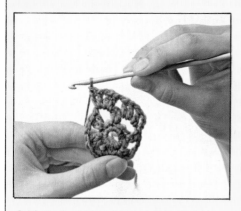

6 Make 1 chain: then work 2 doubles followed by 1 chain and 2 doubles, all into the next chain space in the previous round.

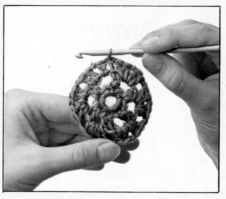

7 Repeat step 6 into each space all the way around the circle. Complete the round with 1 chain and join this with a slip stitch to the top of the first 3 chains. There are now 12 groups of doubles with 1 chain between each. This completes the 3rd round.

8 To begin the 4th round in the correct place, work a slip stitch across the next stitch and into the first chain space so that you will work the first stitch from this space.

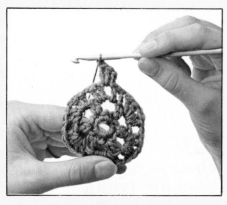

9 Work 3 chains for the first stitch and then 2 doubles into the same space as the first 3 chains making a group of 3 doubles. Now work 1 chain.

10 Continue to work around the circle in the same way, working 3 doubles into each space with 1 chain between each group of doubles.

11 Work the last group of this round into the space before the block of 2 doubles below the first 3 chains. Join last chain to top of first 3 chains with slip stitch.

12 Begin the 5th round by working a slip stitch across the first doubles block of the row below and into the first chain space. Now work 3 chains.

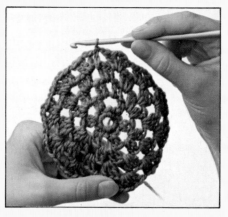

13 Repeat the 3rd round all around the circle, so that there are twenty-four 2-doubles blocks. Join the last chain to the top of the first 3 chains with a slip stitch.

14 To make the motif bigger, repeat the 3rd and 4th rounds alternately until the motif is the required size. To work each round in a different color, break off 1 color at the end of the round and join next color to first chain space of next round. There is no need to work slip stitches at the beginning of the rounds.

Working continuous rounds

An alternative way to work a circle is to crochet continuously around the center circle, leaving the ends of each round unjoined, thus creating a spiral effect on your fabric. By working in this way it is possible to produce a six-sided motif in either a solid fabric — using single crochet or half double — or a more open fabric with a lace pattern incorporated into the design. Try making several motifs, each in a different color, and then sewing them together to make an attractive piece of patchwork. This method of working is frequently used as a form of decorative shaping on the crown of a hat or beret. The lines formed by the increases create a "star" effect on the top of the crown. Our sample has been worked in a knitting worsted with a size G (4.50mm) hook.

1 Make 6 chains and join them to form a circle with a slip stitch. Work 1 chain. Now work 12 single crochets into the center of the circle. Do not join this or any of the following rounds.

2 Now work 2 single crochets into each single crochet of the previous round so that there are 24 stitches in all. Check at this point to make sure you have the correct number of stitches.

3 Now work 1 single crochet into each of the next 3 single crochets of the previous round, and then work 3 chains.

4 Skip the next single crochet and work 1 single crochet into each of the next 3 single crochets. At this point, you have made the first space on the round. Now work 3 chains.

5 Continue to work around the circle in the same way, working 3 single crochets between each space and skipping 1 single crochet below each 3 chains worked until there are 5 chain spaces in all. Complete round by working 3 chains after last 3 single crochets. These chains count as the 6th space on this round.

6 Begin the 4th round by skipping the first single crochet and then working 1 single crochet into each of the next 3 stitches. Now work 2 single crochets into the first 3-chain space on the previous round.

7 Work 3 chains and then 1 single crochet into each of the next 3 stitches, followed by 2 single crochets into the next space. The first space of the 4th round is thus worked to the left of the space in the previous round to begin the spiral shape.

8 Complete this round, working in the same way all around the circle, ending with 3 chains, so that you have worked 5 complete spaces with the last 3 chains counting as the 6th space as before.

continued

Paul Williams

9 Work the 5th round by skipping the first single crochet and working 1 single crochet into each of the next 4 stitches. Now work 2 single crochets into the next space.

10 Work 4 chains and then repeat step 9 once more. Continue to work around the circle in the same way with 4 single crochets between each space, and end the round with 4 chains so that you will have worked 5 complete spaces with the last 4 chains counting as the 6th space as on the previous round.

11 Begin the 6th round by skipping the first single crochet of the next block and working 1 single crochet into each of the next 5 single crochets. Now work 2 single crochets into the next chain space, followed by 4 chains.

12 Repeat step 11 all the way around the circle until you have worked 5 spaces with the last 4 chains counting as the 6th space as before.

13 Work the 7th round by skipping the first single crochet and then working 1 single crochet into each of the remaining single crochets in the next block, followed by 2 single crochets into the next space and then 5 chains. Work in the same way all around the circle, making 5 spaces as before and counting the last 5 chains as the 6th space.

14 Continue to repeat the last round 5 times more to make a motif approx. 8in in diameter, always skipping the first stitch on each block of single crochet in the previous round and then working into each remaining stitch in the block. There will be one more stitch worked in each block on every round.

Making a simple tassel

Follow these step-by-step directions to make the tassel for the blue hat featured on page 9. You can alter the size of the tassel by changing the length of yarn cut and the number of pieces you use.

1 Cut 16 pieces of yarn, each approximately 5in long. Fold the yarn in half.

2 Cut a piece of yarn at least 12in long and tie one end firmly around the center of the lengths of yarn.

Paul Williams

3 Wind the remaining piece of yarn several times around the top of the tassel just below the center fold, leaving enough yarn to be threaded into a needle.

4 Thread the yarn into a blunt-ended needle and insert the needle under the yarn wound around the tassel, and up through the middle of the tassel.

5 Catch the yarn with a slip stitch in the middle of the head of the tassel and then take it down through the center so that it becomes one of the ends. Trim the ends if necessary.

Three crocheted hats

If you've got a head for hats, make up one — or all three — of these crocheted charmers. Worked in rounds, they can be varied in all sorts of ways to team up with just about anything in your wardrobe

Neil Kirk

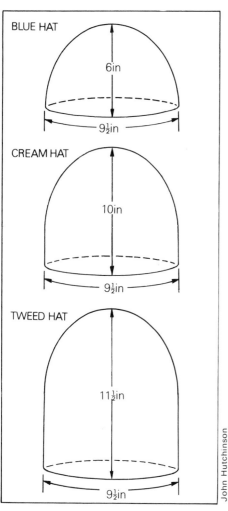

BLUE HAT

6in

9½in

CREAM HAT

10in

9½in

TWEED HAT

11½in

9½in

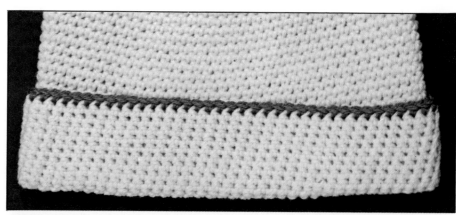

John Hutchinson

Sizes

To fit average size head: these measurements are shown on the diagrams.

Materials

Blue hat *total of 3oz (85g) of knitting worsted*
Cream hat *total of 5oz (145g) of knitting worsted*
Scraps of blue yarn
Tweed hat *total of 4oz (115g) of knitting worsted*
Size E (3.50mm) crochet hook
Size F (4.00mm) crochet hook

Gauge

18sc and 20 rows to 4in (10cm).

Blue hat

*Using size F (4.00mm) hook make 3ch, join with a sl st to first ch to form a circle.
Next round Work 6sc into circle; mark the first of these 6sc to denote the beginning of the round.
Working in continuous rounds, proceed as follows:
Work 2sc into each of next 6sc to increase 6sc.
Work (1sc into next sc, 2sc into next sc) 6 times.

Work (1sc into each of next 2sc, 2sc into next sc) 6 times.
Work (1sc into each of next 3sc, 2sc into next sc) 6 times.
Work (1sc into each of next 4sc, 2sc into next sc) 6 times.
Cont to increase in this way until 11sc have been worked between each increase; you should have 76sc.*
Work straight on these 76sc until work measures 6in (15cm) measured at center.
Change to size E (3.50mm) hook and work 1 round. Fasten off.

Cord

Using size E (3.50mm) hook make 60ch, sl st into each ch to end. Fasten off.
Make 2 tassels and sew one to each end of cord.
Sew center of cord to the top of the hat.

Cream hat

Using cream, work as given for blue hat from * to *.
Work straight on these 76sc until work measures 10in (25cm) measured at center. Fasten off.
With wrong side of work facing join blue and work 1 round of sc. Fasten off.
Turn back 2¼in (6cm) for brim.

Tweed hat

Work as given for blue hat from * to *
Work straight on these 76sc until work measures 11½in (29cm) measured at center.
Fasten off. Fold back 6in (15cm) for brim.

*Making a tubular fabric
*Two textured stitches
*Pattern for a striped bolster
*Pattern for a child's top

Making a tubular fabric

You've already learned to work in rounds, increasing on each round to make a flat motif. If you work in rounds without increasing, you can create a seamless tubular fabric of any width you like, which can be used to make a variety of garments, toys and household items, such as the multi-colored bolster featured on page 15 in this course. The tube is worked onto a basic circle, which should be the same size as the circumference of the article to be made.

Since the right side of the fabric will always be facing you, the stitches appear quite different from the way they look when worked in rows. However, if the work is divided at a given point, such as for the armhole shaping on a sweater, and then completed in rows, you must turn the work at the end of each round so that the stitches will always look the same throughout.

Try our sample using a knitting worsted yarn and size G (4.50mm) hook.

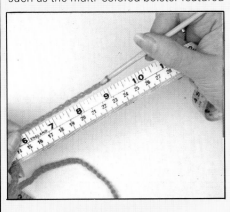

1 Work 45 chains. The length of chain should correspond exactly to the circumference of the circle to be made. Thus, for a child's sweater measuring 23½in (60cm) around the chest, you would need to begin by making a chain 23½in (60cm) long. There is no need to add extra chains for turning.

2 Hold the hook in your right hand. Bring the free end of chain forward and up to the hook. Insert the hook into the first chain made. This prevents the chain from becoming twisted.

3 Wind the yarn over and around hook from back to front and draw it through both loops on the hook to make a slip stitch.

4 Begin the round with the correct number of chains for the stitch being worked—in this case 3 chains for a double. Hold ring to left of hook and work 1 double into the first chain to the left of these first 3 chains.

5 Work 1 double into each following chain all the way around the circle so that you are working in a clockwise direction.

6 Join the last double of the round to the 3rd of the first 3 chains—worked at the beginning of the round—with a slip stitch to complete the first round.

continued

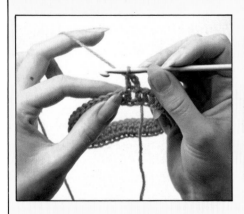

7 Begin 2nd round by making 3 chains. Skip the first double, which is the double at the base of the first 3 chains. Now work 1 double into the next double.

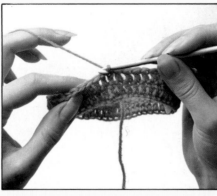

8 Work 1 double into each double all the way around the circle and join last double to top of the first 3 chains as before. By working continuously around the circle in this way you will always have the right side of the fabric facing you.

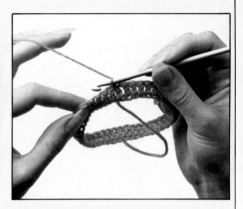

9 Where the fabric is to be divided at a given point the work must be turned at end of each round. Work steps 1 to 6 as before. Do not continue to work around the circle, but turn the work so that the wrong side, or inside, of the tube is facing you.

10 Now make 3 chains. The last stitch of the last round will now become the first stitch.

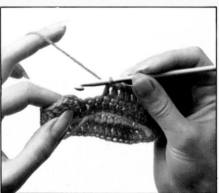

11 Now continue to work the next round as before, working in the same direction.

12 Continue to work as many rounds as required, remembering to join with a slip stitch and to turn the work at the end of each round until the section is completed.

Two textured stitches

Here are two simple textured stitches for you to try. Both are worked in half doubles to give a firm, close fabric. You can make the samples in a knitting worsted using a size G (4.50mm) hook, or try using different yarns and hook sizes to see the varied effects which can be achieved with the same stitch.

Large granite stitch

This stitch should be worked over a number of chains divisible by 2, plus 2 extra chains for the turning.

1 Make 22 chains and work 2 half doubles into 3rd chain from hook. The first chain will count as the first hdc of the row.

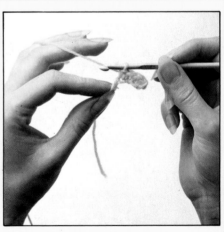

2 Skip the next chain and work 2 half doubles into the next chain.

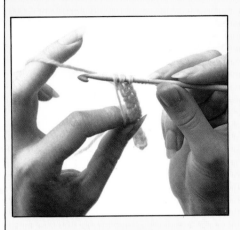

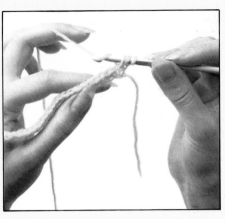

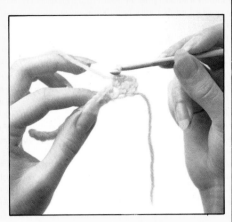

3 Repeat step 2 along the chain until 1 chain only remains unworked. Now work 1 half double into this chain.

4 Turn work. Make 2 chains to count as the first half double. Now work 1 half double between the first stitch at the edge of the work and the first half double group. This will count as the first half double group of the 2nd row.

5 Now work 2 half doubles between 2nd and 3rd half double groups of the previous row.

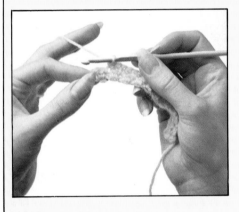

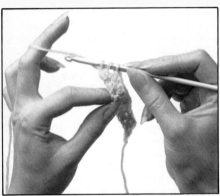

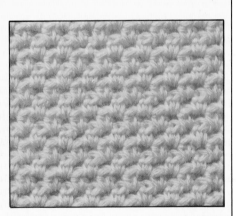

6 Continue to work in the same way as in step 5 between each half double group of the previous row until the last half double group has been reached.

7 Now work 1 half double into the top of the 2 chains at the end of the row, to complete the 2nd row of the pattern.

8 Repeat steps 4 to 7 for every row, always working the first group as in step 4 and the last half double into each turning chain of the previous row.

Crossed half doubles

This stitch makes use of a simple technique to produce a firm, thick fabric. The pattern is worked over a number of chains divisible by 2 plus 2 extra chains for the turning.

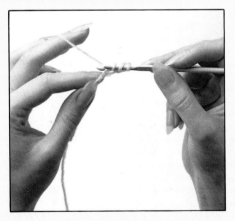

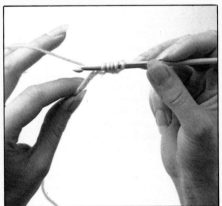

1 Make 22 chains for the base of the pattern. Wind yarn around hook and insert it into 4th chain from hook. Wind yarn around hook again and draw through a loop so that there are 3 loops on the hook.

2 Wind yarn around hook again and insert it into the next chain. Wind yarn around the hook and draw a loop through once more. There are now 5 loops on the hook.

continued

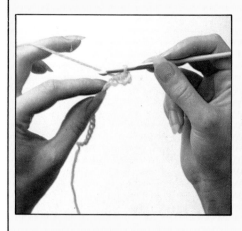

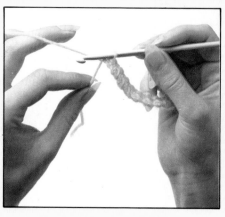

3 Wind the yarn around the hook and draw it through all 5 loops on the hook. You have now made a cluster group over 2 chains.

4 Now work one chain and then work another cluster group in the same way as before over the next 2 chains. Continue to work 1 cluster group over every 2 chains until only one chain remains unworked. Work 1 chain and then one half double into the last chain.

5 Turn the work and make 3 chains which will count as the first half double and 1 chain space. Wind the yarn around the hook and insert the hook into the first 1 chain space of the previous row. Now wind yarn around hook and draw through a loop.

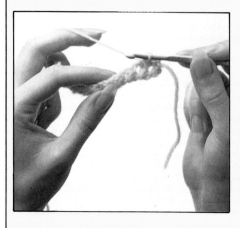

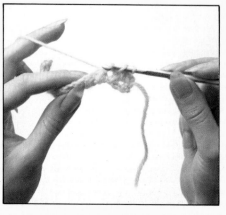

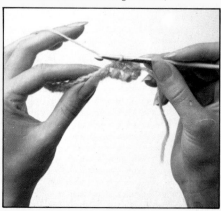

6 Complete the cluster group by working as before into the next 1 chain space in the previous row.

7 Make 1 chain. Now wind yarn around the hook and insert the hook into the same space as the last stitch just worked. Wind yarn around the hook and draw through a loop.

8 Wind yarn around hook and insert into next 1 chain space. Wind yarn around hook and draw through a loop.

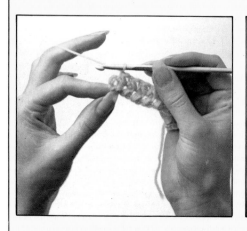

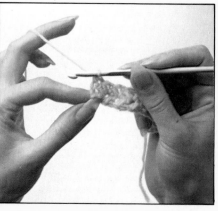

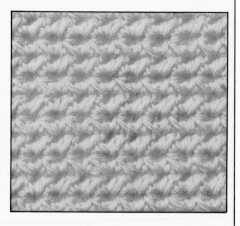

9 Repeat steps 7 and 8 across the row, beginning to work each group in the same space as the last stitch just worked until only the turning chain remains unworked in the previous row.

10 Make 1 chain. Now work 1 half double into the top of the turning chain of the previous row to complete the 2nd row.

11 The 2nd row forms the pattern for this stitch. Repeat it for at least 10 rows to obtain the full effect of this stitch.

A bright way with stripes

You'll enjoy making this big bolster cover with its bright-colored stripes, worked in rounds. It's a simple way to add a decorative—and practical—furnishing to your home.

Caroline Arber

Size
The cover measures 10in (25.5cm) in diameter x 30½in (77.5cm) long.

Materials
Total of 36oz (1000g) of a knitting worsted
Our cover took 12½oz (350g) of green (A), 9oz (250g) of yellow (B) and 14½oz (400g) of rust (C)
Size H (5.00mm) crochet hook
Bolster to fit. The bolster should be approx 1in (2.5cm) larger in diameter and length than cover for a smooth fit.

Gauge
18 sts and 20 rounds to 5in (13cm) worked in hdc on a size H (5.00mm) hook.

To make first circle
Work circle in stripes of 2 rounds A, 2 rounds B and 2 rounds C throughout. Using A, make 6ch, join into a circle with a sl st.
1st round Work 2ch to count as first hdc, now work 10hdc into circle, join with a sl st to 2nd of first 2 ch. 11 sts.
2nd round 2 ch to count as first hdc, 1 hdc into first st; now work 2hdc in to each st around circle, join with a sl st to 2nd of first 2ch. 22 sts.
3rd round 2ch, *1hdc into each of next 2 sts, 2hdc into next st, rep from * 6 times more, 1hdc into st at base of 2ch; join with sl st to 2nd of first 2ch. 30 sts.
4th round 2ch, 1hdc into each of next 2 sts, 2hdc into next st, *1hdc into each of next 3 sts, 2hdc into next st, rep from *5 times more, 1hdc into each of next 2 sts, join with sl st to 2nd of first

2ch. 37 sts.
5th round 2ch, 1hdc into each of next 2 sts, 2hdc into next st, *1hdc into each of next 4 sts, 2hdc into next st, rep from * 5 times more, 1hdc into each of next 3 sts; join with sl st to 2nd of first 2ch. 44 sts.
6th round 2ch, 1hdc into each of next 2 sts, 2hdc into next st, *1hdc into each of next 5 sts, 2hdc into next st, rep from * 5 times more, 1 hdc into each of next 4 sts, join with sl st to 2nd of first 2ch. 51 sts. Cont to increase 7 sts in this way on every round, beginning each round as given for 6th round and working one more st between increases at end of each subsequent round, until 17 rounds have been worked (ending with C) and there are 128 sts. Do not break off yarn.

To make bolster
Cont to work in rounds without increasing to make main part of bolster.
Next round With C 2ch, skip first st, 1hdc into each st all around circle. Join last hdc to top of first 2ch with sl st. 127 sts. Cont to work 7 more rounds in this way in C, then 2 rounds B, 8 rounds A, 2 rounds B, 8 rounds C and 2 rounds B. Do not break off yarn but begin square pattern with it as follows:

Work square pattern
Use separate balls of yarn for each block of color, twisting yarns at back of work when changing colors. Turn work at end of each round, after joining with sl st, so that colors are in correct position when working next round.
1st round With B 2ch, skip first st, work 18 sts A, *3 sts B, 18 sts C, 3 sts B, 18 sts A, repeat from * once more. Now work 3 sts B, 18 sts C and 3 sts B. Join last hdc to 2nd of first 2ch with sl st. Turn. There are 6 large blocks with a small block of B between each. Work 19 more rounds in this way, keeping color pattern correct, and turning work at end of each round. Cut off additional balls of yarn except for last B. Turn work at end of last round so that you will be working striped pattern in correct direction. Now cont to work rounds in stripes of 2 rounds B, 8 rounds A, 2 rounds B, 8 rounds C and 2 rounds B. Repeat square pattern once more, but working C instead of A and vice versa. Turn work once more so that you are working in right direction and work stripe pattern of 2 rounds B, 8 rounds A, 2 rounds B, 8 rounds C, 2 rounds B and 8 rounds A. Draw yarn through and fasten off. Make a 2nd circle as for first, but working A in place of C and vice versa. Fasten off.

To finish
Darn all loose ends of yarn to WS of

Bolster
10in diameter

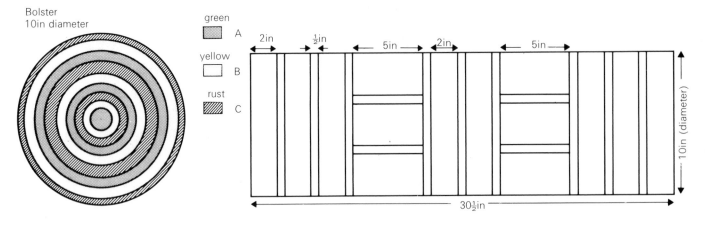

green   A

yellow   B

rust   C

work. Insert bolster in cover. With RS of 2nd circle facing, rejoin A to a hdc on 17th round. Working through both thicknesses, join circle to top edge of bolster with sc. Work round of sc in C through last round of first circle and first

row of tube in same way at other end.

To make your own filling

Roll a piece of foam rubber approx 1in (2.5cm) thick by $2\frac{3}{4}$yd (2.5m) long by $31\frac{1}{2}$in (80cm) wide into a tube approx

11in (28cm) in diameter. Make a tube from a sheet of unbleached calico $33\frac{1}{4}$ in (84cm) by $32\frac{3}{4}$in (83cm) to cover foam rubber, with circle at each end $12\frac{1}{4}$in (31cm) in diameter. (These measurements give you $\frac{5}{8}$in [1.5cm] seam allowances.)

Rounds for applause

For playtime—or anytime—a child needs clothes with lots of "give." This comfortable sweater, crocheted in rounds, is sure to be an all-time favorite.

Size
To fit 20[22:24:26]in (51[56:61:66]cm) chest.
Length, 15[17:18:$19\frac{1}{2}$]in (38[43:46:49]cm).
Sleeve seam, $13\frac{1}{4}$[$14\frac{3}{4}$:$15\frac{1}{4}$:$16\frac{3}{4}$]in (33[36:38:41]cm).

Note the directions for larger sizes are given in brackets []; where there is only one set of figures it applies to all sizes.

Materials
Total of $12\frac{1}{2}$[16:18:$19\frac{1}{2}$]oz (350[450:500:550]g) of a knitting worsted
Size F (4.00mm) crochet hook

Gauge
17hdc and 12 rows to 4in (10cm) worked on a size F (4.00mm) hook.

Back and front (worked in a tubular fabric to armhole).
Chain 96[104:112:120]. Join the last ch to the first with a sl st, taking care not to twist the ch.
Base row 2ch to count as first hdc, skip 1ch, work 1hdc into each ch to end of round. Join with sl st to first ch. Turn.
1st round 2ch, skip first hdc, work 1hdc into each st to end of round. Join with sl st to first ch. Turn. Rep first round throughout, turning the work at the end of each round until 26[30:32:36] rows

in all have been worked. You can adjust the length at this point if necessary.

Divide for back
Work across first 48[52:56:60] hdc, turn. Continue to work in rows on these sts for back with 2 turning chains at the beginning of each row. Work 12[14:16:16] more rows.
Shape shoulders
*Sl st across first 8[9:10:10] sts, cont in patt across row until 8[9:10:10] sts remain unworked, turn and leave these sts for 2nd shoulder. Rep from * once more, then draw yarn through loop on hook and fasten off.
Work front and divide for front opening
Return to remaining sts. Rejoin yarn at armhole edge and pattern across first 24[26:28:30] sts, turn and complete this side first. Work 7[9:11:13] rows.
Shape front neck
Patt across first 20[20:22:24] sts, turn and leave remaining 4[6:6:6] sts unworked.

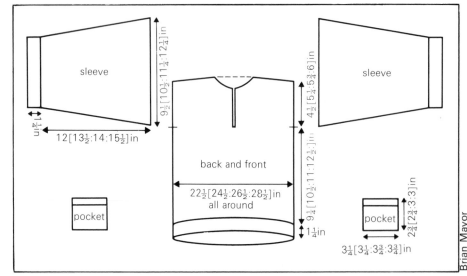

Decrease 1hdc at neck edge on next and every following row (by working 2hdc together one st from neck edge) until 16[18:20:20]hdc remain, ending at neck edge.

Shape shoulder

Work across first 8[9:10:10]hdc, turn and leave remaining 8[9:10:10] sts unworked.

Work 1 more row. Draw yarn through and fasten off.

With right side of front facing, rejoin yarn at front neck opening. Complete the second half of front to match the first, reversing the shaping so that the armhole and neck are worked in the correct position on this side.

Waistband

Rejoin yarn to lower edge of body at side edge.

Next round 1ch, work 1sc into each st all around lower edge of sweater. Join with a sl st first ch. Turn.

Rep this round 4 times more. Draw yarn through. Fasten off.

Sleeves

Join shoulder seams on wrong side of work. With right side of work facing, rejoin yarn to underarm. Work 40[44:48:52] hdc evenly all around armhole; join last hdc to first with sl st, so forming a circle.

Continue in tubular fabric as given for body, decreasing one st at each end of every following 6th[7th:8th:8th] round until 30[34:38:42] sts remain.

Continue without shaping until 36[40:42:46] rounds in all have been worked. You can adjust length here if necessary. Do not cut off yarn.

Cuff

Continue in rounds as before, work 4 rounds in sc. Draw yarn through and fasten off.

Neckband

With right side of front facing, rejoin yarn to right front at neck edge. Work 44[46:48:50]sc evenly around neck edge, ending at left front neck edge. Turn. Work 4[4:5:5] rows in sc on these sts. Do not fasten off. Continue to work 1 row in sc down one side of front opening, up other side and around neck edge again. Fasten off.

Pockets (make 2)

Make 14[14:16:16]ch. Work 8[8:10:10] rows in hdc, then 3 rows in sc on these sts. Fasten off.

To finish

Darn all loose ends in on wrong side of work. Press lightly under a damp cloth with a warm iron. Sew pockets to front. With double thickness of yarn make a chain 35in (90cm) long. Using spaces between stitches at neck edge, lace cord up front opening as shown. Turn back cuff to required depth.

Crochet /COURSE 17

*Making buttonholes
*Chain button loops
*Simple crochet ribbing
*Final list of abbreviations
*Pattern for a man's vest

Making buttonholes

Both horizontal and vertical buttonholes are easy to make—either on the main fabric of your garment or on a separate band which can be sewn on afterward. Your pattern will tell you how many buttonholes you should make for your garment. Before working the buttonholes, you should measure the length of the button band—or the edge of your garment on which the buttons will be sewn—and mark the button positions on it, spacing them at equal distances from each other. Using these marks as a guide, you will know precisely where to make each buttonhole when working the buttonhole band.

Our samples were made with a size G (4.50mm) hook and knitting worsted, and the buttonhole measures approximately $\frac{3}{4}$in (2cm). You can vary the size of the buttonhole by using a different thickness of yarn or a different size hook, or by altering the number of stitches or rows in the buttonhole.

Horizontal buttonholes

1 Make 25 chains and work 4 rows in single crochet. When the buttonholes are being worked on the edge of the main fabric, always make sure that you finish the last row—the one before the buttonhole row—at the center front edge.

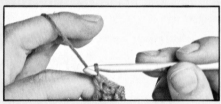

2 Turn and work 3 single crochets. Do not forget to count the turning chain as one stitch. The number of stitches worked at the edge of the fabric will depend on the thickness of yarn being used.

3 Now work 4 chains for the first buttonhole.

4 Skip the next 4 single crochets. Now work 1 single crochet into the next stitch. You can alter the number of chains made and stitches skipped in the row below according to the size of buttonhole required.

5 Now work in pattern to the end of the row. Turn and work back to the point where the buttonhole has been made.

6 Work a single crochet into the stitch just before the chain made in the previous row.

7 Now work 1 single crochet into each chain made in the previous row, placing the hook through the middle of the chain each time. This completes the buttonhole.

8 Now work in pattern to the end of the row. The two buttonhole rows are now completed; there should be the same number of stitches in the row as there were before you worked the hole.

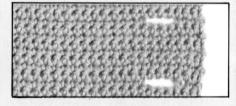

9 Repeat these two rows each time a buttonhole is to be made. If you are making a separate buttonhole band, work the buttonholes in exactly the same way.

Vertical buttonholes

1 For this sample we have used a size G (4.50mm) hook and knitting worsted. Make 17 chains and work 4 rows in single crochet. When working on the main fabric make sure that you always finish the last row—the one before the buttonhole row—at the center front edge.

2 Turn and work 4 single crochets. Do not forget to count the turning chain as one stitch. Now turn and leave the remaining stitches unworked.

3 Work 6 more rows on these 4 stitches for the first side of the buttonhole, so that you finish the last row at the buttonhole edge.

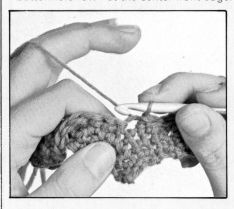 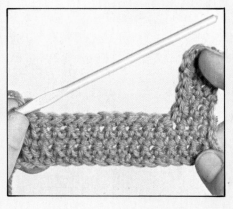 

4 Do not turn. Work in slip stitch down the side of the buttonhole. Work the last slip stitch into the same place as the first single crochet worked for the first side of the buttonhole.

5 Make 1 chain. Now skip 1 stitch and work 1 single crochet into each stitch to the end. Work the last single crochet into the turning chain.

6 Now work 6 more rows on these 12 stitches so that this side has the same number of rows as the other side of the buttonhole. You should finish this row at the side edge of your fabric.

7 Turn and work back to the edge of the buttonhole. Now work 1 single crochet into the edge stitch on the other side of the buttonhole to join the two sides together.

8 Work in pattern to the end of the row to complete the first buttonhole. It is a good idea to count the stitches at this stage to make sure that you have the correct number.

9 Make all the buttonholes in the same way, whether working up the side edge of your fabric, or making a separate band which is to be sewn on afterward.

Fred Mancini

Chain button loops

On some crochet fabrics it is not always necessary to make buttonholes since the spaces between the stitches can be used in place of buttonholes. The tiny buttons used on baby clothes can often be fastened through the fabric. However, if you are working an edging around a garment the depth of the edging may prevent your using the fabric in this way. In this case the simplest way to make a buttonhole is to work crochet loops at evenly spaced intervals down the side of your garment.

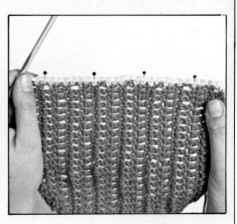

1 Work a row of single crochet down the side of the garment. Your pattern will tell you the stitch you should use and precisely how many rows to work before you make a button loop.

2 On the edge of the garment mark the positions of the loops by counting the stitches to be worked between loops.

3 Work in single crochet to the point where the first button loop is to be made.

4 Now work 3 chains. You can alter the number of chains to make different sized button loops.

5 Skip the next 3 stitches on the previous row, and work 1 single crochet into the next stitch. The number of stitches you skip should always be the same as the number of chains you have just made.

6 Work in single crochet until you reach the marker for the next loop.

7 Now repeat steps 4 and 5 once more to make the second button loop.

8 Continue down the side of the fabric, working the loops in the same way until the edging is completed.

Simple crochet ribbing

Here is a simple form of ribbing, similar in appearance to knitted fisherman's ribbing, especially when worked in a bulky yarn. Although it does not have the same elasticity as knitted ribbing, it is still useful for making collars, cuffs and waistbands. Used for the main fabric of a garment, the stitch makes a really attractive texture which is quick and easy to work.

The method of working differs from the usual way, in that the number of stitches needed to begin the pattern will correspond to the depth of the ribbing required, rather than the width. This means that you are, in effect, working from side to side, rather than from the lower edge to the top, so that it is only when the fabric thus made is turned sideways that the ribbed effect becomes apparent. You work around the garment, rather than starting at the lower edge. Try our sample using a bulky yarn and a size I (6.00mm) hook.

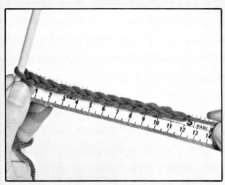

1 Make 13 chains for a piece of ribbing measuring approximately 4¾in (12cm) in depth.

2 Work 1 single crochet into 3rd chain from hook and then 1 single crochet into each chain to the end.

3 Turn, 1 ch. Skip the first single crochet. Insert the hook from front to back into the back, horizontal loop of the next stitch—not under both loops as in ordinary crochet.

4 Draw the yarn through and complete the single crochet in the normal way.

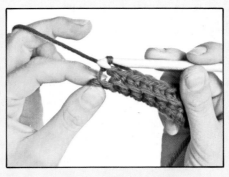

5 Continue to work a single crochet into each stitch, through the back loop only, in the same way until only turning chain remains.

6 Work the last stitch into the back of the turning chain. If you work into the turning chain in the normal way you will find that the edge of your work becomes distorted.

7 Work each row in the same way until the piece is the required length. This should be the same length as the width of the garment you are making.

8 When the ribbing is to be used as a waistband or cuff, turn work at the end of the last row so that the rows just worked now run vertically rather than horizontally.

9 Continue to work along the side edge of the ribbing to begin the main part of the garment, working one stitch into each row end unless your instructions tell you otherwise.

Fred Mancini

Final list of abbreviations

beg=begin(ning)
ch=chain(s)
dc=double crochet
dtr=double triple
foll=follow(ing)
grp(s)=group(s)
hdc=half double crochet
rep=repeat
sc=single crochet
sl st=slip stitch
sp(s)=space(s)
st(s)=stitch(es)
tr=triple crochet

The list on the left gives, alphabetically, the abbreviations you have learned so far. To complete your knowledge of crochet shorthand, we list the remaining commonly-used terms, along with their abbreviations. There are a few more crochet abbreviations for specialized terms, which will be introduced as they arise in the course. From now on, the course patterns will use all the standard abbreviations.

approx=approximately
cont=continu(e) (ing)
dec=decreas(e) (ing)
inc=increas(e) (ing)
patt=pattern
rem=remain(ing)
RS=right side
tog=together
WS=wrong side
yo=yarn over and around hook

Man's vest

This vest is ideal for keeping the winter chill out. It's made of warm sport yarn in an easy-to-work pattern and trimmed with crochet ribbing.

Sizes
To fit 38[40:42]in (97[102:107]cm) chest.
Length, 24[24¾:25½]in (61[63:65]cm).
Note Directions for larger sizes are in brackets []: where there is only one set of figures it applies to all sizes.

Materials
9[10:10]oz (250[275:275]g) of a sport weight yarn
Size E (3.50mm) crochet hook
Size F (4.00mm) crochet hook
5 buttons

Serge Krouglikoff

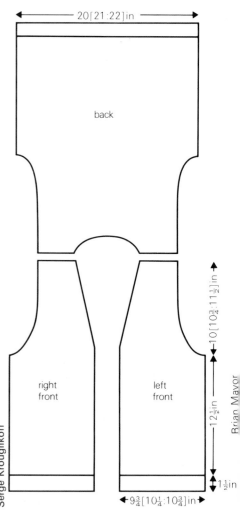

Brian Mavor

Gauge
18 sts and 20 rows to 4in (10cm) over patt worked on a size F (4.00mm) hook.

Back
Using size E (3.50mm) hook make 9ch for side edge of waistband.

Base row 1sc into 3rd ch from hook, 1sc into each ch to end. Turn. 8sts. Commence ribbing.
Rib row 2ch to count as first sc, *1sc into back loop only of next st, rep from* to end. Work last sc into back loop of turning chain. Turn.
Rep the last row 89[93:97] times more. This completes waistband ribbing. Do not turn. Work along one long edge.

Next row 1ch, now work 1sc into each row end all along this edge. Turn. Commence patt.
Next row 2ch, skip first st, *skip next sc, work 2sc into next sc, rep from * to end. Turn.
This row forms the patt and is repeated throughout. Cont in patt until work measures 14in (36cm) from beg.

Shape armholes
Decrease 2sts at each end of next 2 rows, then one st at each end of next 6 rows. 72[76:80]sts. Cont without shaping until armhole measures 10[10¾:11½]in (25[27:29]cm) from beg.

Shape shoulders and neck
Next row Sl st over first 5sts, 2ch to count as first st, now work in patt over first 16[17:18]sts (remember to count the first 2ch as one st). Turn. Complete the right shoulder on these sts.
Next row Decrease one st, patt to last 5sts. Turn. Draw yarn through and fasten off.
Return to remaining sts. With RS of work facing, skip next 30[32:34] sts, rejoin yarn to next st, 2ch, now work in patt to last 5sts, turn and leave these sts unworked.
Next row Sl st over first 5sts, work in patt to last 2sts, work these 2sts together to decrease one st. Draw yarn through and fasten off.

Left front
Using size E (3.50mm) hook ch9. Work

base and ribbing rows as for back. Rep ribbing row 41[43:45] times more. Do not turn but work along one long edge of waistband as for back. 44[46:48]sts. With size F (4.00mm) hook cont in patt as given for back until work measures same as back to armhole, ending at side edge.

Shape armhole and front edge
1st row Sl st over first 2sts, 2ch, patt to last 2sts, work these 2sts together to decrease one st. Turn.
2nd row Work in patt to last 2sts. Turn.
Dec one st at armhole edge on next 6 rows, and *at the same time* decrease one st at front edge on every 3rd row until 20[21:22]sts rem. Cont without shaping until armhole measures same as back to shoulder, ending at armhole edge.

Shape shoulder
Next row Sl st over first 5sts, 2ch, work in patt to end of row. Turn.
Next row Patt to last 5sts, turn and leave these sts unworked.
Draw yarn through and fasten off.

Right front
Work as given for left front, but reversing shaping so that armhole and neck shaping are worked on the opposite side to left front.

Front border
Join shoulder seams on WS with backstitch. With size E (3.50mm) hook and with RS of right front facing, work row of sc up right front, around neck and down left front, working 1sc into each row end. Work 7 rows in ribbing as for back, making 5 buttonholes on 4th row, the first to come approx ⅝in (1.5cm) from the lower edge, with 4 more evenly spaced up left front at approx 3in (7.5cm) intervals as follows:
Work to point where first buttonhole is to be made, make 3ch and skip the next 3sc, cont in patt to the position for the next buttonhole, and work another one in the same way. The last buttonhole should be worked at the point where the front neck shaping begins. On the next row, work 1sc into each of the 3ch made in the previous row to complete the buttonhole. Draw yarn through and fasten off.

Armhole borders
Work as given for front border for 5 rows, omitting buttonholes.

To finish
Press work lightly or block, according to yarn used, omitting ribbing. Join side seams using back stitch seam. Press seams lightly. Sew on buttons to correspond with buttonholes.

Serge Krouglikoff

Shoestring

Letter perfect

This pretty pillow will look just right on your bed—and everyone will know it belongs to you.

Victor Yuan

John Hutchinson

Materials

Three 9½in (24cm)-square handkerchiefs with an initial in one corner

One 9½in (24cm)-square white handkerchief with one decorative corner

Three 12in (30cm)-square handkerchiefs with an initial in one corner

One 12in (30cm)-square plain white handkerchief

One 21½×12in (55×30cm) pillow form

Matching thread

1 Place one small initialed hanky on top of one large initialed hanky, right sides up and with the corners opposite the initials matching, so that both initials are visible. Pin, baste and topstitch together, ⅜in (1cm) from the edge of the smaller hanky.

2 Repeat step 1 with two more pairs of initialed hankies.

3 Place the hanky with the decorative corner on the plain white hanky, right sides up and with the decorative corner of the smaller hanky aligned with one corner of the plain one. Pin, baste and topstitch in place the same as for the initialed hankies.

4 With right sides together and initials matching, place two initialed pairs of hankies together. Pin, baste and stitch together down one edge of larger

hankies, ⅜in (1cm) from initialed edge.

5 Repeat step 4 to sew the third initialed pair of hankies to decorative/plain pair of hankies.

6 Pin, baste and stitch the resulting pairs of hankies together the same way, so the initials and the decorative corner all meet at the center point.

7 Place the hankies over the pillow form diagonally with the initialed center point in the middle of one side of the pillow form and pin it in place.

8 Fold the corners of three of the handkerchiefs to the back of the pillow, leaving one long edge free. Slip stitch edges together. Fold over remaining corner and slip stitch edges to the other handkerchiefs to enclose the pillow form.

Crochet /COURSE 18

Crochet edgings

Crochet edgings are extremely versatile, giving you plenty of scope for adding your individual touch to a garment.

In this course we show you how to work a selection of different edgings directly onto your fabric. These edgings can be used simply to neaten the edge of the fabric (for example, a plain crab-stitch edging on a really bulky garment) or for decorative effect as well (for example, a delicate chain-loop edge around a baby's shawl). The edgings may be worked onto crocheted or knitted fabric, using the same or contrasting colored yarn. It is important, however, to choose a type of yarn and edging appropriate to the garment you have made. Use a fine edging to go around a baby's dress or summer top and a heavier edging for a bulky jacket or coat.

If you are working down the side of your fabric, rather than into each stitch across the row, you may need first to work a row of single crochets to form a firm base for the edging. The numbers of single crochets you work down the row ends depends on the kind of stitch, hook and yarn used for the main fabric. Make sure you do not work too few stitches, as this pulls the edge and distorts the shape.

Crab-stitch edging

This popular and very simple edging is an ideal way to give a firm neat edge to a bulky garment. The finished result is not unlike a form of blanket stitching, and for this reason it is particularly effective when worked in a bulky yarn on a thick fabric.

1 Work 1 row of single crochets as a base row along the edge of your fabric. Work the last single crochet into the corner of the fabric.

2 Do not turn the work as you would normally do. Keep holding the yarn and hook in the same hands as before, with the yarn to the left of the work.

3 You now continue to work back along the row from left to right, rather than from right to left in the usual way. Begin by making 1 chain.

4 Skip the first stitch and insert the hook from front to back into the next stitch. Now place the hook over the yarn.

5 Draw the yarn through and complete the single crochet as usual. Work 1 single crochet into each stitch along the row the same way. Fasten off.

Fred Mancini

Lace-shell edging

This pretty lace edging looks best in a sport yarn or a finer yarn. We show you how to work down the side of the garment, but you can, of course, work across the fabric, working into each stitch rather than each end of row.

1 Work a row of single crochets along the edge of your fabric as a base row for the edging. This will also help to neaten the edge of your fabric.

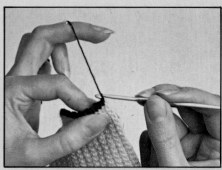

2 Turn the work so that you are ready to work back along the single crochet row in the normal way. Now make 1 chain, skip the first 2 single crochets.

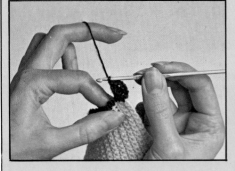

3 Work 2 doubles, then 2 chains and 2 doubles all into the next single crochet. Skip the next 2 single crochets.

4 Repeat step 3 all along the edge of the fabric until only one single crochet remains unworked.

5 Complete the edging by working a slip stitch into the corner of the fabric. Fasten off.

Scalloped-shell edging

This edging is most effective when worked directly onto the fabric, rather than over a base of single crochets. It can be worked either into the stitches across the row or into the end of the rows. It produces a scalloped effect on the edge of the garment.

1 Join yarn to corner. Make one chain. Skip the next row end (or stitch) and work 3 doubles into the following row end to form the first shell shape.

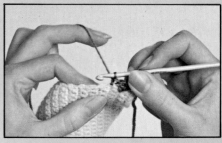

2 Now skip the end of the next row and work 1 single crochet into the end of the following row.

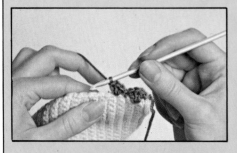

3 Skip the end of the next row and work 3 doubles into the following end of row for the 2nd shell.

4 Continue to repeat steps 2 and 3 all the way across the edge until the last shell has been worked.

5 Now skip the end of the next row and work the last single crochet into the corner of the fabric. Fasten off.

Chain-loop edging

The pretty arched effect of this simple lace edging is achieved by working a series of chain loops on top of each other. You could make the edging deeper by working more chain loops until it is the depth you require.

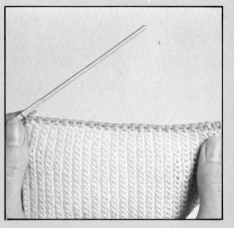

1 Work a base row of single crochets down the side of the fabric. Make sure that you work an even number of stitches for this edging.

2 Turn and work 1 chain to count as the first single crochet. Now work 5 more chains. Skip the next single crochet and work 1 single crochet into the next stitch, thus forming the first arch.

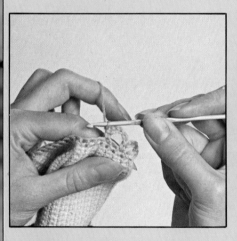

3 Work 5 chains. Skip the next single crochet and work 1 single crochet into the next stitch for the second arch.

4 Repeat step 3 all the way along the row, working the last single crochet into the corner of your fabric.

5 Turn work. Now make 5 chains and then 1 single crochet into center of first 5-chain loop of previous row.

6 Make 5 chains. Now work 1 single crochet into the center of the next 5-chain loop.

7 Continue to repeat step 6 all along the row until only 1 loop remains unworked in the previous row.

8 Work 5 chains as before. Now work a slip stitch instead of a single crochet into the center of the last loop and fasten off the yarn.

Fred Mancini

Sweet and simple

For dress-up occasions, this apron will make a plain dress extra special.

Sizes
To fit 22[24:26]in (56[61:66]cm) chest. Length from shoulder, 18½[20½:22½]in (47[52:57]cm).

Note Directions for larger sizes are in brackets []. Where there is only one set of figures it applies to all sizes.

Materials
5½ [6½:7]oz (150 [175:200]g) of a medium-weight crochet cotton
Size C (3.00mm) crochet hook
2 buttons

Gauge
22 sts and 22 rows to 4in (10cm) in patt worked on a size C (3.00mm) hook.

Skirt
Using size C (3.00mm) hook ch 58 [64:70].
Base row Work 1sc into 4th ch from hook, * now work 1dc into next ch, 1sc into next ch, rep from * to end. Turn. 56[62:68] sts.
Patt row 3ch to count as first dc, skip first sc, * work 1sc into next dc, 1dc into next sc, rep from * to end of row. Work last sc into turning ch, turn. The last row forms the patt and is rep throughout. Cont in patt until work measures 9½[10½:12]in (24[27:30]cm) from beg.

Work edging
Do not turn work, but cont to work down side edge, working 1sc into each row end to lower edge, 1sc into rem loop of each ch along lower edge and 1sc into each row end up other side of work. Fasten off. With RS of work facing rejoin yarn to beg of edging and work 1ch, * skip next sc, work 2dc, 2ch and 2dc all into next sc to make a shell, skip next sc, 1sc into next sc, rep from * around 3 sides as before. Fasten off.

Bib
Using size C (3.00mm) hook ch 30[34: 38]. Work base row and patt row as for skirt. 28[32:36] sts. Cont in patt until bib measures 4¾[5:5½]in (12[13:14]cm) from beg.

Work straps
Patt over first 6[6:8] sts, turn and leave rem sts unworked. Cont on these sts for 12[12¾:13½]in (30[32:34]cm). Fasten off. Return to rem sts. Skip next 16[20:20] sts, rejoin yarn to next st and work in patt to end of row.
Complete as given for first strap.

Edging
Work edging as given for skirt along outer edges of bib and straps, and then along inner edge of first strap, across top of bib and along inner edge of 2nd strap. Fasten off.

Waistband and ties
Using size C (3.00mm) hook ch 9. Work 1sc into 3rd ch from hook, 1sc into each ch to end. Turn. 8 sts. Cont to work in sc until band measures 37[39:41]in (95[100:105]cm) from beg. Fasten off.

Pocket
Using size C (3.00mm) hook ch 18 [22:26]. Work base row and patt row as for skirt. 16[20:24] sts. Cont in patt until pocket measures 2¾[3:3½]in (7[8:9]cm) from beg.
Shape lower edge
Next row 1ch, 1sc into each of next 3 sts, * skip next dc, 1sc into each of next 3 sts, rep from * to end so that only 13[16:19] sts rem.
Next row 1ch, skip 1[0:0]sc, * work 2dc, 2ch and 2dc and 2sc, all into next sc, skip next sc, 1sc into next sc, skip next sc, rep from * 1[2:3] times more, work 2dc, 2ch and 2dc all into next sc, skip 1[1:0]sc, 1sc into turning ch. Fasten off.

To finish
Press work lightly under a damp cloth with a warm iron. Sew lower edge of bib to center of waistband. Sew top of skirt to other side of waistband, gathering top slightly. Sew a button 2¾in (7cm) from each side of waistband and make a loop at end of each strap to fasten. Sew on pocket. Press seams.

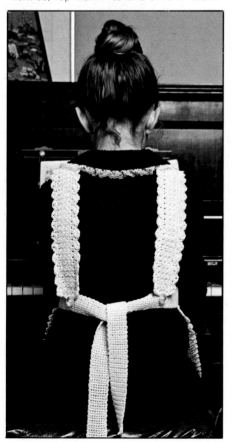

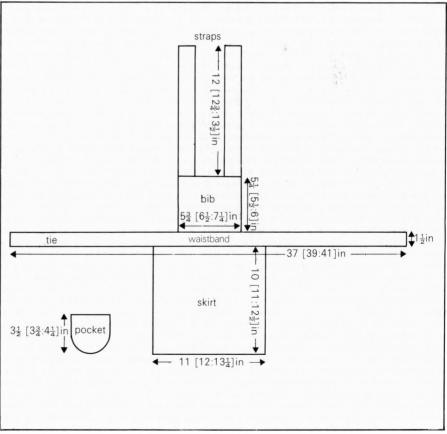

*More T-shaped designs for adult sizes
*Multiple increasing and decreasing at beginning of rows
*Using a circular needle for working in rows
*Sewing on patch pockets
*Making a twisted cord
*Patterns for T-shaped garments

More T-shaped designs for adult sizes

Kim Sayer

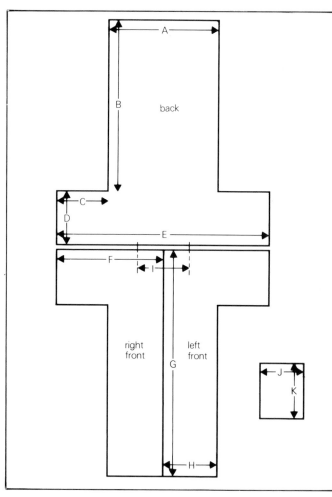

The adaptable T-shape can be used as the basis for many sweater and jacket designs. On pages 35–36 we offer designs for two adult sweaters.

These designs develop the T-shape idea one stage further than in the basic children's designs given earlier. They include pockets and – in the case of the man's sweater – a collar.

If you like, you can adapt designs in a variety of ways – by using a different stitch, by altering the proportions or by

Bust /chest size for jacket (in)	Code	32	34	36	38	40
Width across back	A	17	18	19	20	21
Underarm length	B	19¼	19¾	20	20½	20¾
Sleeve length	C	14½	15¼	16¼	17	17¾
Armhole depth	D	7	8	8¾	9½	10¼
Width sleeve edge to sleeve edge	E	46	48½	51½	54	56½
Width from sleeve edge to center front	F	23	24¼	25¾	27	28¼
Total length of jacket	G	26½	27½	28¾	30	31
Width across front	H	8½	9	9½	10	10½
Width of neck opening	I	7½	7½	8	8¼	8¼
Pocket width	J	4¾	5	5½	6	6¼
Pocket depth	K	6	6¼	6¾	7	7½

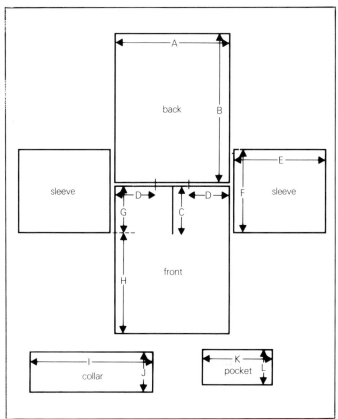

Brian Mayor

adding or subtracting a collar or pockets. The diagrams and measurements given here are slightly more detailed than those included with the pattern and may be used as a guide in adapting the designs, if you so choose. Making minor adjustments on a simple pattern is a good way to begin learning the basics of pattern design.

If you want to use a different stitch, remember to make a gauge sample using your chosen yarn and needles. Use the measurement chart to determine the number of stitches to cast on and bind off in shaping the garment.

If you are altering one measurement in the garment, remember to take into consideration the effect this could have on another part of the garment. For example, if you want to widen the neck opening on the man's sweater you must also increase the width of the collar so that it will fit around the entire neck edge. You may also want to increase the depth of the collar.

Similarly, a pocket should also vary in size according to the garment. If you prefer to substitute two patch pockets for the single horizontal pocket on the man's pullover, you should first complete the front piece, then make two paper patterns and lay them on the finished piece of knitting to check their size. Trim the patterns if necessary, and knit the pockets to that measurement.

Bust/chest size for sweater (in)	Code on diagram	32	34	36	38	40	42
Width across front/back	A	17	17¾	19	20	21	22
Total length of sweater	B	22½	23½	24¾	26	27¼	28¼
Depth of front opening	C	6¾	7½	8¼	9	9¾	10½
Shoulder seam (from each side edge)	D	4¾	5	5½	6	6¼	6¾
Sleeve length	E	14½	15¼	16	17	17¾	18½
Width all around sleeve	F	13½	15	16½	18	19¾	21½
Armhole depth	G	6¾	7½	8¼	9	9¾	10½
Underarm length front/back	H	15¾	16	16½	17	17¼	17¾
Collar width	I	14¼	15	15¾	16½	17¼	18
Collar depth	J	8	8	8	8	8	8
Pocket width	K	7	7	7	9	9	9
Pocket depth	L	5¼	6	6	6¾	6¾	7½

On some T-shaped designs the sleeve and bodice are knitted in one piece, as on the women's jacket. You can apply this technique to other T-shaped designs. There are two ways of knitting the sleeve and the bodice in one piece. If you are knitting the garment from bottom to top, you proceed as usual up to the armhole point, then cast on the required extra stitches for the length of each sleeve. You then continue knitting across the entire width from one wrist to the other (measurement "E" on the diagram) until you reach the upper edge. Alternatively, if you are knitting the garment sideways, you cast on the required number of stitches for the sleeve width, knit the sleeve, then cast on the required extra stitches for the bodice front and back. You then continue knitting across the bodice (binding off, if necessary, for a front opening), bind off the bodice stitches at the side seam and complete the other sleeve.

Multiple increasing and decreasing at beginning of rows

Sometimes a pattern will include a design feature that requires you to cast on or bind off a number of stitches at a time. For example, garments in which the sleeves are worked in one piece with the body involve this multiple increasing and decreasing in order to form sleeve or side edges, depending on the direction of the knitting.

Essentially the same technique is used in making a center front slit for a neckline, as illustrated in the following steps.

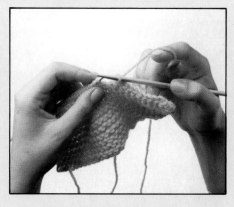

1 To make an opening for the neck in a fabric being knitted sideways, bind off the required number of stitches at the beginning of a row in the usual way. One stitch remains on the right-hand needle.

2 Work to the end of the row. The first stitch (the one remaining on the right needle after binding off) counts as one of the stitches in that row.

3 Now, work the following row (the bound off stitches will be to your left). Transfer the needle with the stitches to your left hand (shown above) to start the next row.

4 Using the two-needle method (see Volume 1, page 26), cast on the number of stitches required. For an opening, the cast on stitches must correspond in number to those bound off previously.

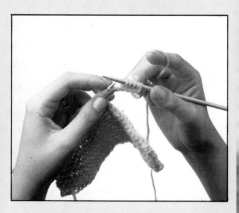

5 Work into each of the cast on stitches, then continue knitting across the main piece of fabric.

Using a circular needle for working in rows

A circular needle consists of two short rigid needles joined by a length of flexible nylon wire. This type of needle is generally used for working in rounds to form a seamless piece of knitting but it also has advantages in flat knitting (that is, working backward and forward in rows).

Whenever you have a large number of stitches in a piece of knitting, the work eventually becomes heavy and unwieldy; when most of a row has been worked, the needle holding the new stitches is difficult to handle. A circular needle can hold a great number of stitches; and because there is only one needle, the weight of the work is evenly distributed between both hands.

1 When making a garment from cuff edge to cuff edge, use an ordinary pair of needles to make the sleeves and to cast on stitches for side seams. On the next row, transfer the stitches to a circular needle; use one point of the circular needle in your right hand and knit in the usual way.

2 At the end of the row, when all the stitches are on the circular needle, transfer the point with the stitches to your left hand. The opposite side of the work must be facing you for the next row — in this case it is a purl row.

3 Work stitches from left needle point to right in the usual way. Once the right-hand needle is full of stitches move them to the wire.

4 During the course of a row you will need to keep a constant supply of stitches to be worked on the left-hand needle. Move the stitches along the wire accordingly.

5 After each row, turn the work around so that the opposite side is facing for the next row, in the same way as in using a pair of needles. Continue in this way for the depth you require : bind off stitches in the usual way.

Sewing on patch pockets

Patch pockets are easy to make in a variety of stitches : they are simply squares or rectangles knitted separately from the main garment and sewed on later. The pocket must, however, be sewed on correctly so that it looks neat and attractive. Don't rely on your eye to place the pocket on the fabric accurately ; follow the pointers given here for a professional finish.

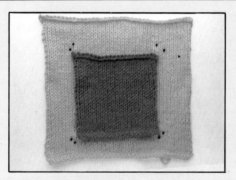

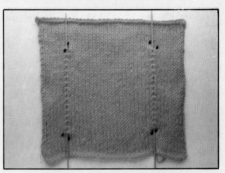

1 Make a pocket of the required size and bind off as usual. Position the pocket on the main fabric and mark the corners with pins. Remove the pocket for the time being.

2 Check that the pins run in straight lines along the rows and stitches. Use fine knitting needles, pointed at both ends, to pick up alternate stitches of the main fabric just outside the vertical lines of pins. This is a useful guide for a straight edge.

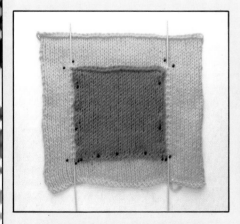

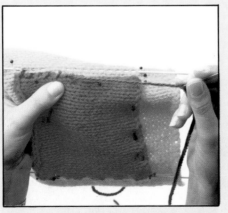

3 Pin pocket in position just inside the knitting needles. Check that the lower edge runs across a straight line of stitches on the main fabric.

4 Thread a blunt-ended yarn needle with matching yarn (we have used a contrasting color for clarity) and secure to back of work. Overcast the pocket to the main fabric around three sides, taking one stitch from the edge of the pocket and one stitch from the needle alternately down sides of pocket.

5 The finished pocket is sewed neatly in position. Strengthen each side of opening with a few stitches worked over the first line of overcasting.

Paul Williams

Making a twisted cord

For this simple trimming, strands of yarn are twisted together to form a cord; the cord varies in thickness according to the quality of yarn and number of strands used.

Fine cords make pretty and inexpensive ties on babies' garments, and because they are round, they are more comfortable than ribbon. Threaded through eyelet holes, a cord makes an effective drawstring on many kinds of garments. Fine yarns are suitable for cords on evening wear; thicker yarns and more strands make sturdy ties for outdoor clothes. Make an extra-thick cord to form the handle of a tote bag.

Usually, cords are made in the same yarn as the garment itself. You can experiment with different-colored strands of yarn—perhaps including a different texture – to obtain some unusual effects.

1 Cut the required number of strands of yarn; we have used three. Each strand must be three times the length of the finished cord (i.e. 36in [90cm] long to make a 12in [30cm] cord). Knot the strands about ¾in (2cm) from each end.

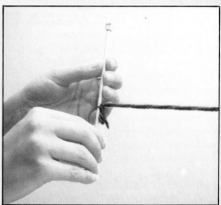

2 Insert a small knitting needle through each knot. Enlist the help of a friend for the next operation. Each of you should take one end of the strands and stand facing each other. Use the knitting needles to twist the strands in a clockwise direction.

3 Keep turning – for what seems like ages – until the strands are tightly twisted and it is impossible to turn any more without the cord twisting back on itself.

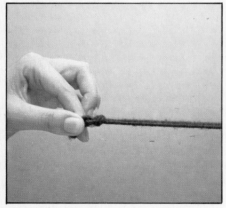

4 Still holding the strands and keeping them taut, fold them in half at the center. Without letting go of the ends, remove the knitting needles and knot the two ends together just above the previous knots.

5 Hold the knot and give the cord a sharp shake; smooth it down from the knot to the folded end to even out the twists.

6 Undo the original knots at the ends of the strands and even out the yarn in the tassel. Neaten the tassel by trimming ends. If you are using the cord as one of a pair of ties, sew the folded end to the garment.

7 To use the cord as a drawstring, make another tassel at the folded end. Knot the cord, leaving enough length at the end to make a matching tassel. Cut through the loops and smooth out the ends.

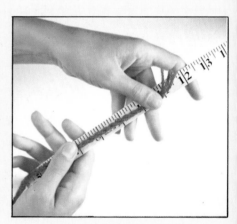

8 The finished cord is about one third the length of the original strands of yarn, including the tassels.

Paul Williams

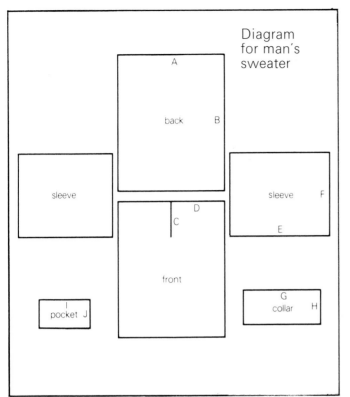

Diagram for man's sweater

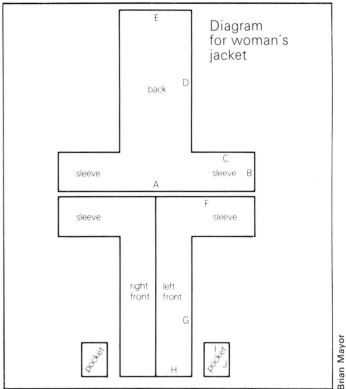

Diagram for woman's jacket

Brian Mayor

T-shape for two

Here are two more clever ways with the versatile T-shape pattern. The man's sweater and woman's jacket are worked in garter stitch in bulky yarn. Patch pockets are good looking and practical.

Woman's T-shaped jacket

Sizes
To fit 32[34:36:38:40:42]in (83[87: 92:97:102:107]cm) bust: other measurements are shown on the chart, right.

Note instructions for larger sizes are in brackets []: where there is only one set of figures, it applies to all sizes.

Materials
36[38:39:41:43:45]oz (1000[1050: 1100:1150:1200:1250]g) of bulky yarn
½oz (10g) of knitting worsted in a contrasting color for trimming
No. 10 (6½mm) knitting needles
No. 10 (6½mm) circular needle
Size F (4.00mm) crochet hook

Gauge
14 sts and 28 rows to 4in (10cm) over garter st on No. 10 (6½mm) needles.

Back
Using No. 10 (6½mm) needles and bulky yarn, cast on 60[63:67:70:74:77] sts and work in garter st for 19¼[19¾:20:20½: 20¾:21¼]in (49[50:51:52:53:54]cm).
☐ For the sleeves, cast on 51 [54:57:60: 63:66] sts at beg of next 2 rows. 162[171:181:190:200:209] sts.
☐ Change to No. 10 (6½mm) circular needle and continue in garter st until work measures 26½[27½:28¾:30:31:32¼]in (67[70:73:76:79:82]cm) from beg. Bind off.

Left front
Using the pair of No. 10 (6½mm) needles and bulky yarn cast on 30[32:34:35:37: 39] sts and work in garter st for same length as back to sleeves.
☐ For the sleeve, cast on 51 [54:57: 60:63:66] sts at beg of next row. 81 [86:91:95:100:105] sts.
Continue in garter st until work is same length as back. Bind off.

Right front
Work as given for left front; the work is reversible.

Pockets (make 2)
Using the pair of No. 10 (6½mm) needles and bulky yarn, cast on 21 [22:24:25:27: 29] sts and work in garter st for 4¾[5:5½: 6:6¼:6¾]in (12[13:14:15:16:17]cm). Bind off.

To finish
☐ Do not press.
☐ Join upper sleeve and shoulder seams by overcasting, leaving 7½[7½:8:8¼:8¼: 8¾]in (19[19:20:21:21:22]cm) free for neck. Join side and underarm seams by overcasting.

Measurements for woman's T-shaped jacket
(see diagram above)

A	46(48½:51½:54:56½:59)in
B	7(8:8½:9½:10¼:11)in
C	14½(15¼:16¼:17:17¾:18½)in
D	19¼(19¾:20:20½:20¾:21¼)in
E	17(18:19:20:21:22)in
F	23(24¼:25¾:27:28½:29½)in
G	26½(27½:28¾:30:31:32¼)in
H	8½(9:9½:10:10½:11)in
I	4¾(5:5½:6:6¼:6¾)in
J	6(6¼:6¾:7:7½:7¾)in

☐ With right side facing, join knitting worsted and work a row of single crochet evenly all around outer edge.
☐ With wrong side facing, work single crochet around lower edge of sleeves.
☐ Turn back 4in (10cm) at lower edge of each sleeve to form cuff.
☐ Work single crochet around the four edges of pockets, then sew pockets to fronts, placing one edge at side seam and leaving top two-thirds of this side open.
☐ Using 4 strands of knitting worsted, make two twisted cords each about 20in (50cm) long and sew one to each front to tie as shown in picture overleaf.

Kim Sayer

Man's T-shaped sweater

Sizes
To fit $32\frac{1}{2}$[34:36:38:40:42]in (83[87:92:97:102:107)cm) chest: other measurements are shown on the diagram (page 31) and corresponding chart, right.
Note instructions for larger sizes are in brackets []; where there is only one set of figures it applies to all sizes.

Materials
50[53:53:57:57:60]oz (1400[1500:1500:1600:1600:1700]g) of bulky yarn
1 pair No. 9 (6mm) knitting needles

Gauge
16 sts and 32 rows to 4in (10cm) over garter st on No. 9 (6mm) needles.

Back (worked sideways)
Using No. 9 (6mm) needles cast on 91[96:101:106:111:116] sts for side edge. Work garter st for 17 [$17\frac{3}{4}$:19:20:21:22]in (43[45:48:51:53:56]cm). Bind off.

Front (worked sideways)
Using No. 9 (6mm) needles cast on 91[96:101:106:111:116] sts for side edge. Work garter st for $8\frac{1}{2}$ [$8\frac{7}{8}$:$9\frac{1}{2}$:10:$10\frac{1}{2}$:11]in (21.5[22.5:24:25.5:26.5:28]cm).
Next row Bind off 28[31:34:37:40:43] sts for neck opening, K to end of row.
Next row K to end, then turn and cast on 28[31:34:37:40:43] sts for neck opening. 91[96:101:106:111:116] sts.
☐ Continue in garter st until front measures same as back. Bind off.

Sleeves (worked from wrist)
Using No. 9 (6mm) needles cast on 54[61:67:74:80:87] sts and work in garter st for $14\frac{1}{2}$[$15\frac{1}{4}$:16:17:$17\frac{3}{4}$:$18\frac{1}{2}$]in (37[39:41:43:45:47]cm). Bind off.

Collar
Cast on 32[32:32:32:32:32] sts and K 2 rows.
Next row (Right side) K6, then (P4, K4) to the last 2 sts, K2
Next row K2, P4, (K4, P4) to the last 2 sts, K2.
☐ Rep these 2 rows until work measures $13\frac{3}{4}$[$14\frac{1}{2}$:$15\frac{1}{4}$:16:17:$17\frac{3}{4}$]in (35[37:39:41:43:45]cm) from beg, ending with a right-side row.
☐ K2 rows, then bind off.

Pocket
Cast on 32[32:32:40:40:40] sts.
Work the 2 rows of K4, P4 ribbing with 2 sts at each end in garter st as given for collar for $5\frac{1}{4}$[6:6:$6\frac{3}{4}$:$6\frac{3}{4}$:$7\frac{1}{2}$]in (13[15:15:17:17:19]cm). Bind off loosely.

To finish
☐ Do not press.
☐ Join shoulder seams for $4\frac{3}{4}$[5:$5\frac{1}{2}$:6:$6\frac{1}{4}$:$6\frac{3}{4}$]in (12[13:14:15:16:17]cm).
☐ Mark center of sleeve top edge with a pin: match pin to shoulder seam and join sleeves to body by overcasting.
☐ Join side and sleeve seams by overcasting.
☐ Sew cast-on edge of collar to neck.
☐ Sew on pocket, sewing along cast-on and bound-off edges. Press seams.

Measurements for man's T-shaped sweater
(see diagram on page 35, top left)

A	17($17\frac{3}{4}$:19:20:21:22)in
B	$22\frac{1}{2}$($23\frac{1}{2}$:$24\frac{3}{4}$:26:$27\frac{1}{4}$:$28\frac{1}{4}$)in
C	$6\frac{3}{4}$($7\frac{1}{2}$:$8\frac{1}{4}$:9:$9\frac{3}{4}$:$10\frac{1}{2}$)in
D	$4\frac{3}{4}$(5:$5\frac{1}{2}$:6:$6\frac{1}{4}$:$6\frac{3}{4}$)in
E	$14\frac{1}{2}$($15\frac{1}{4}$:16:17:$17\frac{3}{4}$:$18\frac{1}{2}$)in
F	$13\frac{1}{2}$(15:$16\frac{1}{2}$:18:$19\frac{3}{4}$:$21\frac{1}{2}$)in
G	$14\frac{1}{4}$(15:$15\frac{3}{4}$:$16\frac{1}{2}$:$17\frac{1}{4}$:18)in
H	8(8:8:8:8:8)in
I	7(7:7:9:9:9)in
J	$5\frac{1}{4}$(6:6:$6\frac{3}{4}$:$6\frac{3}{4}$:$7\frac{1}{2}$)in

Knitting /COURSE 16

*The advanced T-shape
*Working a neck shaping
*Usine a pair of needles to
  pick up stitches around neck
*Finishing off a crew
  neckband
*Honeycomb slip stitch
*Pattern for a
  T-shaped sweater

The advanced T-shape

The sweater included in this course is more advanced in style than the basic T-shapes included in previous courses. This design features a shaped neck finished with a crew neckband or turtle-neck collar to make it sit comfortably around the neck. It also has a ribbed waistband to draw in the lower edge and ribbed cuffs so that it fits the body more closely.

The diagram and measurement plan give a whole range of children's and adults' sizes. If you want to add neck shaping to the T-shaped designs shown in previous chapters, refer to the chart on this page and find measurements G, H, I and J for the size you are making. Calculate the number of stitches and rows on the shaping using the instructions given in Knitting Course 14, Volume 3, page 48.

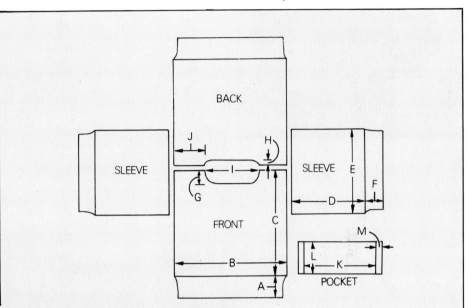

Basic measurements for designing T-shaped sweater (in inches)

Chest/bust sizes	Code	20	22	24	26	28	30	32½	34	35	38	40	42
Depth of waistband	A	$1\frac{1}{4}$	$1\frac{1}{2}$	$1\frac{1}{2}$	2	2	2	2	$2\frac{3}{8}$	$2\frac{3}{8}$	$2\frac{3}{4}$	$2\frac{3}{4}$	$2\frac{3}{4}$
Width across front/back	B	11	12	13	11	15	16	17	18	19	20	21	22
Length from waistband to shoulder	C	$10\frac{1}{4}$	11	$13\frac{1}{4}$	15	$16\frac{1}{2}$	18	$19\frac{3}{4}$	$21\frac{1}{4}$	$22\frac{3}{4}$	$23\frac{1}{2}$	$24\frac{1}{2}$	$25\frac{1}{4}$
Sleeve length from cuff to top	D	7	$8\frac{3}{4}$	$10\frac{1}{4}$	$11\frac{1}{2}$	$12\frac{1}{2}$	$13\frac{3}{4}$	$14\frac{1}{2}$	$15\frac{1}{4}$	16	$16\frac{1}{2}$	$17\frac{1}{4}$	18
Width all around sleeve	E	$10\frac{1}{4}$	11	$11\frac{3}{4}$	$12\frac{1}{2}$	$13\frac{1}{4}$	$14\frac{1}{4}$	15	$15\frac{3}{4}$	$16\frac{1}{2}$	$17\frac{1}{4}$	18	19
Depth of cuff	F	$\frac{3}{4}$	$\frac{3}{4}$	$\frac{3}{4}$	$1\frac{1}{4}$	$1\frac{1}{4}$	$1\frac{1}{4}$	$1\frac{1}{2}$	$1\frac{1}{2}$	$1\frac{1}{2}$	2	2	2
Depth of front neck shaping	G	2	2	2	$2\frac{1}{4}$	$2\frac{1}{4}$	$2\frac{1}{4}$	$2\frac{3}{4}$	$2\frac{3}{4}$	$2\frac{3}{4}$	$3\frac{1}{4}$	$3\frac{1}{4}$	$3\frac{1}{4}$
Depth of back neck shaping	H	$\frac{3}{8}$	$\frac{3}{8}$	$\frac{3}{8}$	$\frac{5}{8}$	$\frac{5}{8}$	$\frac{5}{8}$	$\frac{3}{4}$	$\frac{3}{4}$	$\frac{3}{4}$	1	1	1
Width of front/back neck	I	6	$6\frac{1}{4}$	$6\frac{1}{2}$	$6\frac{3}{4}$	7	$7\frac{1}{4}$	$7\frac{1}{4}$	$7\frac{1}{2}$	$7\frac{3}{4}$	8	$8\frac{1}{4}$	$8\frac{1}{2}$
Shoulder seam	J	2	$2\frac{1}{4}$	$2\frac{3}{4}$	$3\frac{1}{4}$	$3\frac{1}{2}$	4	$4\frac{1}{4}$	$4\frac{3}{4}$	5	$5\frac{1}{2}$	6	$6\frac{1}{4}$
Width of pocket	K	$6\frac{1}{4}$	$6\frac{1}{4}$	$6\frac{1}{4}$	7	7	7	8	8	8	$8\frac{3}{4}$	$8\frac{3}{4}$	$8\frac{3}{4}$
Depth of pocket	L	4	4	$4\frac{3}{4}$	$4\frac{3}{4}$	$5\frac{1}{2}$	$5\frac{1}{2}$	$6\frac{1}{4}$	$6\frac{1}{4}$	7	7	8	8
Width of pocket border	M	$\frac{3}{8}$	$\frac{3}{8}$	$\frac{3}{8}$	$\frac{5}{8}$	$\frac{5}{8}$	$\frac{5}{8}$	$\frac{3}{4}$	$\frac{3}{4}$	$\frac{3}{4}$	1	1	1
Depth of crew neck (after folding in half)		$\frac{5}{8}$	$\frac{5}{8}$	$\frac{5}{8}$	$\frac{3}{4}$	$\frac{3}{4}$	$\frac{3}{4}$	1	1	1	$1\frac{1}{4}$	$1\frac{1}{4}$	$1\frac{1}{4}$
Depth of turtleneck		4	4	$4\frac{3}{4}$	$4\frac{3}{4}$	$5\frac{1}{2}$	$5\frac{1}{2}$	$6\frac{1}{4}$	$6\frac{1}{4}$	7	7	8	8

continued: The advanced T-shape

A shaped neck usually requires some kind of finished edge to make it fit well. This is usually a ribbed neckband—a turtleneck is simply an extended neckband—which is worked directly on the fabric by picking up the stitches around the neck.

A waistband can be added to T-shaped designs by one of two methods depending on the direction of the knitting. If you are working from the lower edge to the top, just cast on the required number of stitches with needles two sizes smaller than those used for the main fabric. Work the depth of ribbing you want—see the chart on page 37—then change to the larger needles and continue in pattern. If you are knitting the sweater sideways, first make the main front and back pieces. Later, pick up stitches along the lower edge for the waistband and work downward in rib to the depth you require.

The number of stitches to cast on for a ribbed cuff is slightly more difficult to calculate. Refer to the chart on page 37 and find the number to cast on for the sleeve edge of an existing T-shaped design. You should cast on approximately two-thirds of this number for the cuff. Again, use needles two sizes smaller than for pattern, and end with a right-side row. Now knit one more row of ribbing (wrong side), increasing to obtain the number of stitches required for the sleeve; do this evenly across the row. To increase by one-third, increase on every other stitch. (See the detailed pattern row given in the directions on pages 41-42 for precise details for making the pullover.)

Working neck shaping

Most patterns give detailed directions on how to work any neck shaping. Here we explain the general principle of the technique. Our sample is the front of a garment and shows how to divide the work and retain stitches for working at a later stage with the aid of an extra needle and stitch holder. In some patterns the center front stitches may be bound off and neckband stitches picked up from this edge rather than holding them on an extra needle as described here.

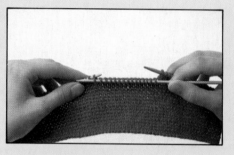

1 Work to point where shaping is to begin. (Usually, as here, you end with a wrong-side row.) On the next row, pattern the required number of stitches for one side of the neck. Leave the remaining stitches on an extra double-pointed needle, there are too many stitches to fit onto a holder. Buy special stops to keep the stitches from falling off the ends, or improvise with corks or rubber bands.

2 Turn the work for the next row. Complete one side of the neck first Here, the left side has been completed, as the piece is the front of the work. If you're making the back you normally complete the right side first. A series of decreased stitches at the neck edge produces a shaping line from the front neck to the shoulder.

3 Return to the stitches on the extra needle; a number of these across the center front neck are left unworked until you add the neckband. With right side of work facing you, begin at the right-hand edge of the stitches on the extra needle and slip the required number for the center front onto a holder.

4 Transfer the stitches still remaining on the extra needle to one of a pair of needles starting at the left-hand edge. You are now ready to begin knitting the right side of the front neck shaping, beginning with a right side row. Rejoin the yarn to inner end of sts on needle and work to the end of the row (armhole edge).

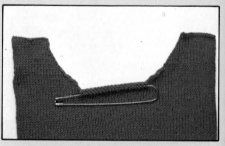

5 Complete the second side of the neck to match the first. Precise directions may be given in the pattern; if not, reverse the neck shaping by decreasing at the right edge instead of the left edge.

Using a pair of needles to pick up stitches around neck

It is possible to make a separate neckband and sew it to the garment, but this may produce a hard, bulky seam across the throat. To prevent this, use the technique of picking up the stitches at the neck edge and knitting the neckband or collar directly onto the garment.

Join one shoulder seam only before beginning the neckband, in this way the back and front open out flat and you can pick up the stitches with a pair of needles instead of with a circular needle or a set of four needles, which are slightly more difficult to use. The needles used for a neckband are usually two sizes smaller than those used for the main fabric.

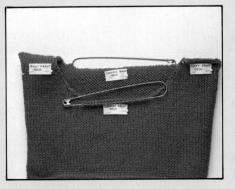

1 Take the front and back sections of the garment and join the right shoulder seam. Turn the work right side out and hold it so that the front is on top, the unjoined shoulder seam is to your right.

2 With the right side of the work facing you, begin picking up stitches for neckband at the left front (un-seamed) shoulder. Insert the left-hand needle from front to back through the first vertical loop of a stitch at end of row.

3 Hold your yarn ready for knitting, leaving an end of about 4in (10cm). Insert the right-hand needle into the loop on left-hand needle, wind the yarn around the right-hand needle tip in the usual knit position and draw a stitch through the loop on the left-hand needle.

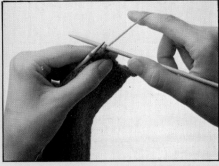

4 There is now one stitch on the right-hand needle. Insert the left-hand needle into the next long vertical loop to the left and pick up another stitch.

5 Continue picking up stitches in this way until you reach the shaped section (on some patterns, the shaping goes right up to the shoulder). The decreased stitches form a sloping loop, insert the left-hand needle into this loop. In general pick up one stitch for every 2 row ends on a shaped edge.

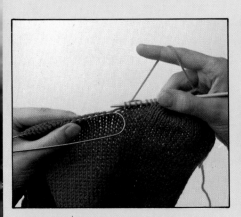

6 Pick up and knit stitches down left front neck until you reach center front neck stitches on holder. Transfer the stitches to the left-hand needle, open the stitch holder at the left edge and, working from left to right, slip the stitches onto the needle one by one.

7 When all the center front neck stitches are on the left needle, knit across them in the usual way.

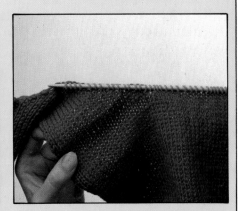

8 Continue around neck, picking up and knitting stitches up right front neck and down right back neck, knitting across center back neck stitches on holder and picking up and knitting stitches up left back neck so that all stitches are on one needle.

Finishing off a crew neckband

For a professional finish and a comfortable fit around the neck, a crew neckband should be worked to twice the required depth and then folded over to the inside. Pick up stitches around neck (with right shoulder seamed) and work in ribbing to twice the depth that you require. Bind off very loosely. Join the shoulder seam that was left open; also join the ends of the neckband in a continuous line with the shoulder seam. The neckband now forms a complete circle.

1 Fold the neckband in half to the wrong side of the work. The bound-off edge is very pliable so that you can easily stretch it to fit all around the inner neck edge. Pin the edge in position exactly on top of the ridges where stitches were picked up around neck.

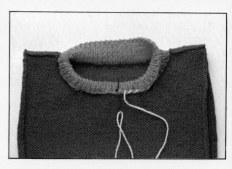

2 Thread a blunt-ended yarn needle with matching yarn — a different color has been used here for clarity. Slip stitch the edge of the neckband in position, taking care that the ridges are just hidden.

Honeycomb slip stitch

This is another useful basic stitch pattern. It produces a neat, textured fabric with an allover honeycomb effect. You can use this stitch pattern as a substitute for garter stitch, stockinette stitch, seed stitch and others when you are designing your own T-shaped sweaters. Remember to work a gauge sample first; although the stitch may substitute for other stitches this doesn't mean that it is equal in gauge to them.

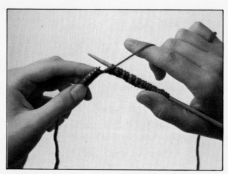

1 Cast on an uneven number of stitches (e.g. 17, 19, 21). To work the first row, P the first st, insert the needle into the next st as if to purl it and transfer it to the right needle without working it — called sl 1 as to purl; P1, alternately sl 1 as to purl, then P1 to the end of the row.

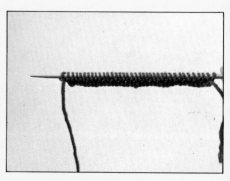

2 Purl each stitch in the 2nd row. Here the wrong side of the work is facing you.

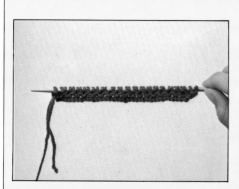

3 To work the 3rd row, P2 sts, then sl 1 as to purl, P1 st alternately until you reach the last stitch; P1 st. This is the right side of the work.

4 Purl the 4th row. Repeat these 4 rows until the fabric is the depth you require. Bind off, preferably, on a wrong-side (i.e. purl) row.

5 The finished fabric has horizontal strands of yarn on the right side formed by passing over slipped stitches. The alternating positions of strands of yarn and purled stitches throughout the fabric creates a three-dimensional texture similar to a honeycomb.

Final list of abbreviations

beg = begin(ning)
dec = decreas(e)(ing)
inc = increas(e)(ing)
K = knit
P = purl
patt = pattern
rem = remain(ing)
rep = repeat
st(s) = stitch(es)
tog = together

On the left is an alphabetical list of knitting abbreviations that you have learned so far. To complete your knowledge of knitting shorthand, the remaining abbreviated terms are given on the right (there are a few more special knitting abbreviations : these will be introduced with the techniques to which they apply). From now on patterns will include the full range of abbreviations.

approx = approximately
foll = follow(ing)
RS = right side
sl = slip
tbl = through back of loop(s)
WS = wrong side

T-shaped sweaters for all the family

Here's a pattern to please every member of your family—an easy-to-wear sweater in the easy-to-make T-shape. A whole range of sizes is given, and you can choose either a crew neck or a turtleneck to finish off the sweater

Sizes
To fit 21[22:24:26:28:30:32:34:36:38: 40:42]in (53[56:61:66:71:76:81:86:92: 97:102:107]cm) chest/bust. Directions for larger sizes are in brackets [], where there is only one set of figures it applies to all sizes.

Materials
Total of 8[10:11:13:14:15:16:18:19: 21:22:23]oz (225[275:325: 375:400:425:450:525:550: 600:625:650]g) of sport yarn
For turtleneck, allow an extra 1[1:1:1:2:2:2:2:3:3:3:3]oz (25[25: 25:25:50:50:50:50:75:75:75:75]g)
1 pair each Nos. 4 (3½mm) and 5 (4mm) knitting needles

Gauge
24 sts and 40 rows to 4in (10cm) in patt worked on No. 5 (4mm) needles.

Back
Using No. 4 (3½mm) needles cast on 67[73:79:85:91:97:103:109:115:121: 127:133] sts.
Beg and ending 1st row with K1 and 2nd row with P1, work 2 rows K1, P1 ribbing. Rep these 2 rows for 1½[1½:1½: 2:2:2:2:2⅜:2⅜:2¾:2¾:2¾] in (4[4:4:5:5:5: 6:6:6:7:7:7]cm) ending with a 2nd row. Change to No. 5 (4mm) needles. Cont in honeycomb slip stitch (see page 40) until work measures 11½[13:14½: 16¼:18:19½:21¼:23:24½:25½:26¼: 27]in (29[33:37:41.5:45.5:49.5:54:58: 62:64.5:66.5:68.5]cm) from beg ending with a P row. Beg neck shaping on next row: patt 16[18:21:24:27:29:33:35:38: 41:44:46]sts, turn and leave rem sts on an extra needle.
Cont in patt, dec one st at beg (neck

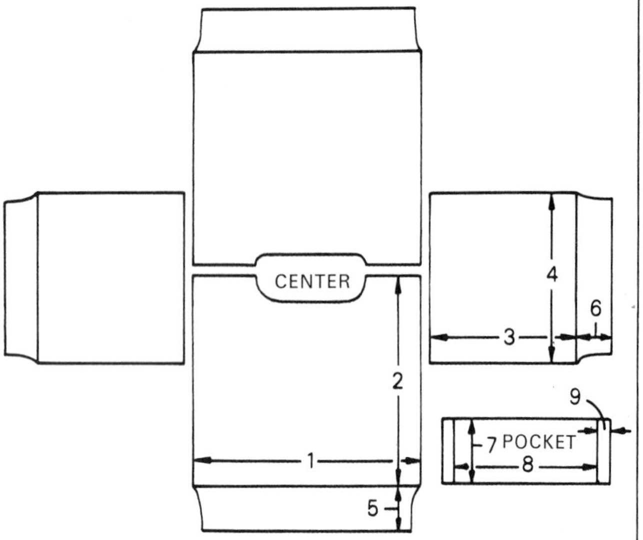

Code	Measurements
1	11[12:13:14:15:16:17:18:19:20:21:22]in
2	10¼[11¾:13¼:15:16½:18:19¾:21¼:22¾:23½:24½:25¼] in
3	7[8¾:10¼:11½:12½:13¾:14½:15¼:16:16½:17¼:18]in
4	10¼[11:11¾:12½:13¼:14¾:15:15¾:16½:17¼:18:19]in
5	1½[1½:1½:2:2:2:2:2⅜:2⅜:2¾:2¾:2¾]in
6	¾[¾:¾:1¼:1¼:1¼:1½:1½:1½:2:2:2]in
7	4[4:4¾:4¾:5½:5½:6¼:6¼:7:7:8:8]in
8	6¼[6¼:6¼:7:7:7:8:8:8:8¾:8¾:8¾]in
9	⅜[⅜:⅜:⅝:⅝:⅝:¾:¾:¾:1:1:1]in

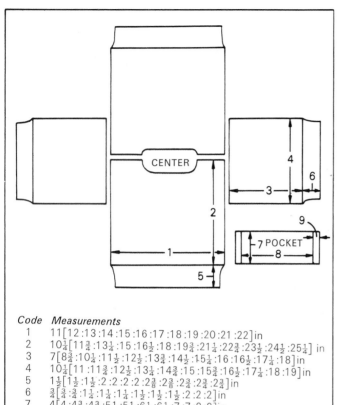

John Hutchinson

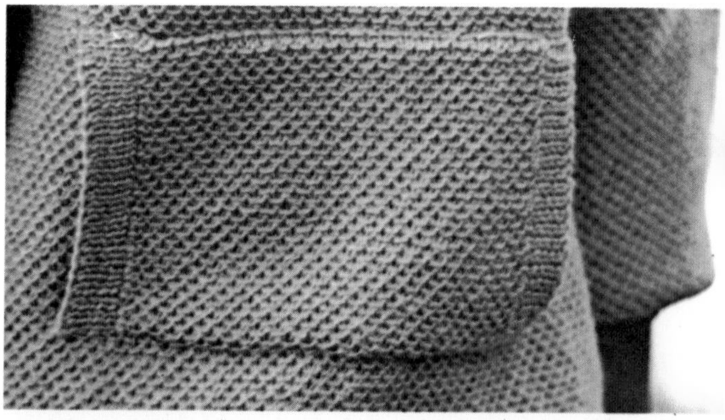

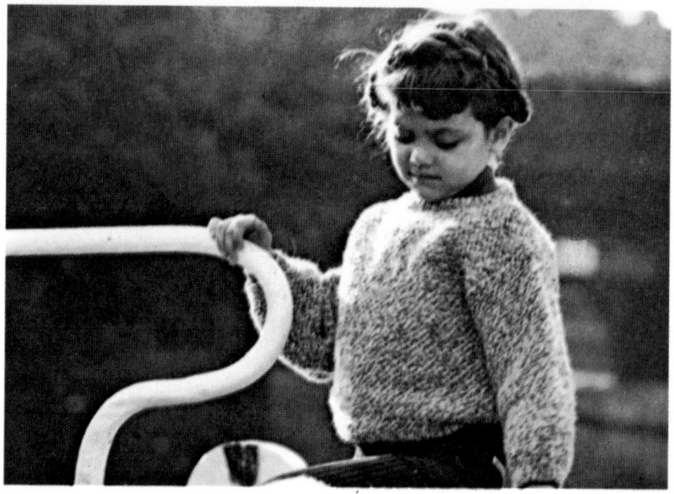

Herb Schmitz

edge) of next and every other row 1[1:1:2:2:2:3:3:3:4:4:4] times, ending with a P row.
Bind off rem 14[16:19:21:24:26:29:31:34:36:39:41] sts.
Return to sts on extra needle; sl first 35[37:37:37:37:39:37:39:39:39:39:41] sts onto a holder for back neck, rejoin yarn to next st and patt to end.
Cont in patt, dec one st at end (neck edge) of next and every other row 1[1:1:2:2:2:3:3:3:4:4:4] times, ending with a P row. Bind off.

Front

Work as given for back until front measures 9¾[11½:13:14½:16¼:17¾:19¼:20¾:22½:23¼:24:24¾]in (25[29:33:37:41:45:49:53:57:59:61:63]cm) from beg ending with a P row.
Beg neck shaping on next row: patt 23[25:28:31:34:36:41:43:46:49:52:54] sts, turn, leave rem sts on extra needle.
Bind off 2 sts at beg (neck edge) of next and every other row 1[1:1:1:1:1:2:2:2:2:2:2] times, then dec one st at same edge on every other row 5[5:5:6:6:6:6:6:6:7:7:7] times.
Cont without shaping until front measures same as back to shoulders, ending with a P row.
Bind off rem 14[16:19:21:24:26:29:31:34:36:39:41] sts.
Return to sts on extra needle; sl first 21[23:23:23:23:25:21:23:23:23:23:25] sts onto holder for front neck, rejoin yarn to next st and patt to end.
P one row, then cont to match the first side.

Sleeves

Using No. 4 (3½mm) needles cast on 41[45:47:51:53:57:61:65:67:71:73:77] sts. Work ¾[¾:¾:1¼:1¼:1¼:1½:1½:1½:2:2:2]in (2[2:2:3:3:3:4:4:4:5:5:5]cm) as given for back, ending with a 1st row and inc one st at end of last row on 3rd-6th and 9th-12th sizes.
Inc to width of sleeve on next row: P1[1:2:2:0:0:1:1:2:2:0:0] sts, then P twice into next st and P1 st alternately to end of row. This makes 61[67:71:77:81:87:91:97:101:107:111:117] sts.
Change to No. 5 (4mm) needles. Cont in honeycomb slip stitch until work measures 7¾[9½:11:12¾:13¾:15:16:16¾:17½:18½:19¼:20]in (20[24:28:32:35:38:41:43:45:47:49:51]cm) from beg.
Bind off very loosely.

Pocket

Using No. 5 (4mm) needles cast on 39[39:39:43:43:43:47:47:47:51:51:51] sts. Work 4[4:4¾:4¾:5½:5½:6¼:6¼:7:7:8:8] in (10[10:12:12:14:14:16:16:18:18:20:20] cm) in honeycomb slip stitch.
Bind off.
Work pocket borders: using No. 4 (3½mm) needles and with RS of work facing, pick up and K 29[29:35:35:41:41:47:47:53:53:59:59] sts along side edge of pocket.
Work ⅜[⅜:⅜:⅝:⅝:⅝:¾:¾:¾:1:1:1]in (1[1:1:1.5:1.5:1.5:2:2:2:2.5:2.5:2.5] cm) ribbing as for back. Bind off in ribbing.
Rep along other side edge.

Neckband

Join right shoulder seam. Using No. 4 (3½ mm) needles and with RS of work facing, pick up and K 16[16:17:19:19:19:22:22:23:25:25:25] sts down left front neck, K front neck sts from holder, pick up and K 15[15:16:18:18:18:21:21:22:24:24:24] sts up right front neck, 3[3:4:5:5:5:7:7:8:9:9:9] sts down right back neck, K back neck sts on holder, then pick up and K 3[3:4:5:5:5:7:7:8:9:9:9] sts up left back neck. This makes 93[97:101:107:107:111:115:119:123:129:129:133] sts.
Cont in K1, P1 ribbing, work 1¼[1¼:1¼:1½:1½:1½:2:2:2:2½:2½:2½] in (3[3:3:4:4:4:5:5:5:6:6:6] cm) for crew neck or 4[4:4¾:4¾:5½:5½:6¼:6¼:7:7:8:8] in (10[10:12:12:14:14:16:16:18:18:20:20]cm) for turtleneck. Bind off in ribbing.

To finish

Block according to yarn used, pressing lightly.
Join left shoulder seam and neckband reversing seam on top half of turtleneck.
Fold crew neckband in half to inside and slip stitch in position.
Mark center of bound-off sleeve edge with a pin; match pin to shoulder seam and sew sleeves in position.
Sew on pocket along top, bottom and lower side edges.
Join side and sleeve seams.
Press seams.

*Understanding a knitting pattern
*Making buttonholes in a ribbed border
*Sewing on a ribbed border
*Setting in a sleeve
*Pattern for a woman's V-neck cardigan

Understanding a knitting pattern

Although the style in which knitting patterns are presented varies slightly according to the publisher, most patterns have certain basic similarities. A pattern is normally divided into three different sections: information about sizes, materials and gauge, working directions for each section and directions for assembling the sections. Full use is made of the abbreviations you already know, and the language is very concise, in order to give a maximum of information in a small space. From this point onward the patterns in the Knitting Course will be written in normal knitting style.

To help the knitter, everything is written in logical order. Read the pattern through before you begin knitting, so that you have a general understanding of the work. Don't worry if a particular detail or direction isn't crystal clear at first reading; many techniques only become obvious when you have the work in front of you.

Sizes

These usually include the chest or bust sizes and other major measurements: scale drawings given in some patterns help you to see at a glance the number of pieces and their measurements. Check the finished lengths of individual pieces and read the working instructions to see if they allow you to make any alterations. A pattern is usually given in a variety of sizes: directions for the larger sizes are in brackets. Read through the complete pattern and circle the figures relevant to your size.

Materials

This section states the amount, brand and quality of yarn used for the garment shown in the photograph. In our patterns, the general type of yarn is quoted, as it is not always possible for the reader to obtain a specific brand. Remember that the quantity of yarn stated is approximate; you may need slightly more or less yarn depending on the brand chosen.
Also listed under "materials" is everything else you will need for the pattern, from knitting needles to zippers.

Gauge

Every pattern gives the recommended gauge that you need to achieve in order to make an item of the correct size. Always make a gauge swatch before you begin, whether you use the original yarn or a substitute.

Directions

Directions for each section of the garment are given under the appropriate headings: "back," "front," and so on. Work the pieces in the order in which they appear in the directions; different pieces may have to be joined before you can continue knitting, or specific directions may be given in full in the first section and referred to more briefly later on in the pattern.
An asterisk, *, is often used to avoid repetition; in a pattern row it means that

you should repeat the sequence of stitches from that point as instructed. A whole section of directions may be marked with single or double asterisks at the beginning and end: these must be repeated at a later stage in the pattern; for example: "Back: work as given for front from * to *."

Finishing

Pay particular attention to this section; it is easy to spoil a beautifully knitted garment by careless finishing. Here you will find details for pressing the yarn; however, if you have used a substitute yarn, you should follow the instructions on the ball band instead.
The pattern directions also tell you the order in which pieces should be sewn together to form the base for any final edgings or trimmings—details of which are also included here.

Abbreviated version

1st row (RS) K2, *yo, K1, yo, sl 1, K1, psso, K9, K2 tog, yo, K1, yo, K3, rep from * to end, but finish last rep K2 instead of K3. 241 sts.
2nd row P5, *P2 tog, P7, P2 tog tbl, P9* rep from * to end, but finish last rep P5 instead of P9. 217 sts.

Here is proof of the practicality and economy of knitting pattern language. This excerpt from a Stitch by Stitch knitting pattern for a Shetland shawl (above left) is only seven lines long. Written out in normal English (on the right), the same directions occupy 17 lines. The final effect (right) is the same.

Full length version

First row (Right side) knit 2, yarn over, knit 1, yarn over, slip 1, knit 1, pass slipped stitch over, knit 9, knit 2 together, yarn over, knit 1, yarn over, knit 3. Repeat this sequence of stitches—beginning with the first "yarn over"—to the end of the row, but on the last repeat knit 2 instead of 3. You now have a total of 241 stitches on the needle.

Second row Purl 5, purl 2 together, purl 7, purl 2 together through the backs of the loops, purl 9. Repeat this sequence of stitches—beginning with the first "purl 2 together"—to the end of the row, but on the last repeat, purl 5 instead of 9. You now have a total of 217 stitches on the needle.

Making buttonholes in a ribbed border

A buttonhole is made by binding off a number of stitches in the center of one row (the number varying with the size of the button) and replacing them with the same number of stitches in the following row. Work as neatly as possible, otherwise you will spoil the appearance of the garment. Patterns tell you precisely how to make the buttonholes and the distance to work between each one. On a garment such as the V-neck cardigan on page 47, the first buttonhole is just above the lower edge, the last level with the beginning of the front edge shaping and the others evenly spaced between them.

1 Cast on the number of stitches specified; in the cardigan pattern it is 10. Work in ribbing until you reach position for the first buttonhole, ending with a wrong-side row.

2 The first buttonhole row reads "rib 4 sts, bind off 2 sts, rib to end." Work the first 4 stitches to reach the bind-off position: rib two stitches, then lift the first over the second in the usual way.

3 Rib 1 more stitch, binding it off in ribbing. On the right-hand needle are 4 stitches before bound-off group and one stitch remaining from binding off.

4 Work to the end of the row; there should be the same number of stitches on each side of the buttonhole. On the 2nd buttonhole row, rib up to the last stitch before the bound-off group.

5 Cast on the same number of stitches as those bound off in the previous row, by increasing into the front and back of the next stitch. Make the first stitch by knitting into the front of the next stitch.

6 Do not drop the stitch you are working into from the left-hand needle. Twist the right-hand needle to the right and behind the left-hand needle: make the next stitch by knitting into the back of the stitch on the left-hand needle.

7 Increase again by knitting into the front of the same stitch. You now have 2 extra stitches on the right-hand needle—the number bound off in last row. (If more stitches have been bound off, continue increasing alternately into the front and back of the same stitch until you have the required number.)

8 Work in ribbing to end of row. On the next row, which is on right side of work, continue in ribbing pattern to end. Work in correct ribbing sequence over cast-on stitches in the center.

Sewing on a ribbed border

Ribbed borders, worked separately, are often used to finish a knitted edge. Usually the edge you are finishing off consists of the row ends at the sides of a piece of knitting such as those along the front opening of a cardigan or jacket. Often, say on a V-neck cardigan, the border fits up one front edge, then extends around the entire neck and down the other front; this type of border may include buttonholes and forms a base for sewing on buttons.

Following the pattern, work border on smaller needles than the main fabric, just as you would for a waistband or cuffs (which are normally knitted in one piece with the main fabric). Make the border very slightly shorter than the edge. Check the gauge by holding it against the edge. Now stretch the border on to the edge before pinning and sewing it in position: this helps to keep the knitting firm and prevent it sagging.

1 Before sewing on the border, block the main piece of knitting. With right side of border (if there is one) against right side of fabric, stretch border slightly to fit edge. Pin along outer edge.

2 Use a blunt-ended yarn needle threaded with matching yarn (we have used a contrasting yarn for clarity) to work a flat seam. Work through edge stitches on both pieces of knitting.

3 If you open the work flat with wrong side facing and gently ease the stitches apart you will see that this type of seam makes a laced effect through the stitches.

4 This is the finished seam on the right side of the work. The yarn used for stitching makes regular, neat bars across the seam: these are indistinguishable when worked in a matching yarn.

Paul Williams

Setting in a sleeve

Setting a sleeve into a garment is an important part of the finishing. Two different shapes must be fitted together; this requires some skill and practice in order to obtain a neat finish.

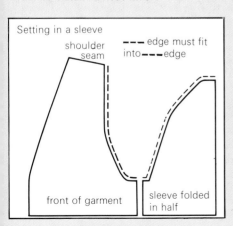

Setting in a sleeve
shoulder seam
- - - edge must fit
into - - - edge
front of garment
sleeve folded in half

1 Join shoulder and side seams on back and front of garment in the usual way. Leave garment wrong side out.

2 Join the sleeve seam and turn the completed sleeve right side out. Fold the sleeve in half with the seam forming one side edge. Mark the center of the sleeve top on the opposite edge to the seam with a pin. *continued*

3 Position sleeve in armhole. With right side of sleeve to right side of garment, match underarm seams and pin. Also match pin at center of sleeve top to shoulder seam and secure with a pin.

4 Always working on edge just inside *sleeve top* (on wrong side of fabric), pin sleeve in position all around; match any decreased edges at underarm and ease in fullness on sleeve top if necessary.

5 Sew sleeve in position with a back-stitch seam, following the line of pins inside the sleeve top edge. The finished sleeve fits neatly into the armhole without puckering. Press gently on the right side of the work if so instructed.

Perennial favorite

Here's a cardigan you ll wear again and again and never tire of. Gently shaded bouclé yarn gives textural interest to its classic lines and makes it extra soft. You can dress it up or down to suit almost any occasion.

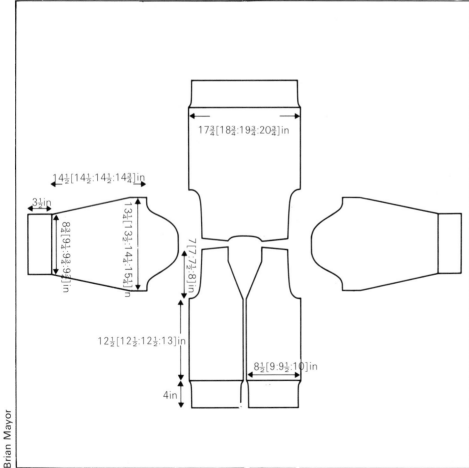

Brian Mayor

Sizes
To fit 32[34:36:38]in (83[87:92:97]cm) bust.
Length, 23½[23½:24:25]in (60[60:62:63]cm).
Sleeve seam, 18[18:18:18¼]in (45[45:45:46]cm).
Note Directions for larger sizes are in brackets [ ]; where there is only one set of figures it applies to all sizes.

Materials
14[16:16:18]oz (400[450:450:500]g) of a medium-weight bouclé yarn
1 pair each Nos. 4 and 7 (3¾ and 5mm) knitting needles
5 buttons

Gauge
16sts and 30 rows to 4in (10cm) in garter st on No. 7 (5mm) needles.

Left front
****Using No. 4 (3¾mm) needles cast on 33[35:37:39]sts.
1st row (RS) K2, *P1, K1, rep from * to last st, K1.
2nd row *K1, P1, rep from * to last st, K1. Rep these 2 rows for 4in (10cm). End with a 2nd row and inc one st at end of last row. 34[36:38:40]sts. Change to No. 7 (5mm) needles. Cont in garter st until work measures 16½[16½:16½:17] 42[42:42:43]cm from beg, ending with a WS row.**
Shape front edge
Next row K to last 2sts, K2 tog, K5 rows.
Shape armhole
Next row Bind off 2[3:3:4]sts, K to last 2sts, K2 tog.
K 1 row. Dec one st at front edge on every 6th row from previous dec, *at same time* dec one st at armhole edge on

next 3 rows, then on every other row 2[2:3:3] times. Keeping armhole edge straight, cont to dec at front edge only until 17[18:19:20]sts rem. Cont without shaping until armhole measures 7[7:7½:8]in (18[18:19:20]cm) from beg, ending at armhole edge.

Shape shoulder
Bind off at beg of every other row 4[5:4:5]sts once, 4[4:5:5]sts twice and 5sts once.

Right front
Work as given for left from ** to ** but inc at beg instead of end of last row of ribbing.
Shape front edge
Next row K2 tog, K to end. K 5 rows.
Next row K2 tog, K to end.
Shape armhole
Next row Bind off 2[3:3:4]sts, K to end. Complete to match left front, working 1 more row before shaping shoulder.

Back
Using No. 4 (3¾mm) needles cast on 69[73:77:81]sts. Work 4in (10cm) ribbing as for left front, ending with a 2nd row and inc one st at each end of last row. 71[75:79:83]sts. On No. 7 (5mm) needles, cont in garter st until back measures same as fronts to armholes, ending with a WS row.
Shape armholes
Bind off 2[3:3:4]sts at beg of next 2 rows. Dec one st at each end of next 3 rows, then on every other row 2[2:3:3] times. Cont straight until armholes measure same as fronts. End with WS row.
Shape shoulders and back neck
Bind off 4[5:4:5]sts at beg of next 2 rows.
Next row Bind off 4[4:5:5]sts, K until there are 12[12:13:13]sts on right-hand needle, bind off next 17sts, K to end. Cont on last set of sts as foll:
1st row Bind off 4[4:5:5]sts, K to last 2sts, K2 tog.
2nd row K2 tog, K to end.
3rd row As first.
K 1 row. Bind off rem 5sts.
Rejoin yarn to rem sts at neck edge.
1st row K2 tog, K to end.
2nd row Bind off 4[4:5:5]sts, K to last 2sts, K2 tog.
3rd row As first.
Bind off rem 5sts.

Sleeves
Using No. 4 (3¾mm) needles cast on 35[37:39:39]sts.
Work 3½in (9cm) ribbing as for left front, ending with a 2nd row.
On No. 7 (5mm) needles, cont in garter st, inc one st at each end of 9th and every foll 10th[10th:10th:8th] row until there are 53[55:57:61]sts. Cont without shaping until sleeve measures

Caroline Arber

18[18:18:18¼]in (45[45:45:46]cm) from beg, ending with WS row.
Shape top
Bind off 2[3:3:4]sts at beg of next 2 rows. Dec one st at each end of next and every other row until 21sts rem, then at each end of every row until 13sts rem. Bind off.

Border
Join shoulder seams. Using No. 4 (3¾mm) needles cast on 10sts.
1st row K2, *P1, K1, rep from * to end. This row forms ribbing. Work 3 more rows.
1st buttonhole row Rib 4sts, bind off

next 2sts, rib to end.
2nd buttonhole row Rib to end, casting on 2sts over those bound off in the previous row.
Make 4 more buttonholes in this way with 3¼in (8cm) between each. Cont to rib until border, when slightly stretched, fits up right front, across back of neck and down left front. Bind off in ribbing.

To finish
Press lightly, following directions on ball band. Sew border in position. Join side and sleeve seams. Set sleeves into armholes. Press seams lightly. Sew on buttons.

Shoestring

Hangers on

Knit one, crochet one—each makes a little sachet that wil[l] impart a sweet fragrance to your closet.

Di Lewis

Materials

Small amount of knitting worsted
1 pair No. 4 (3¾mm) knitting needles
or size E (3.50mm) crochet hook
Small amount of potpourri
Small amount of stuffing, (absorbent
cotton, synthetic stuffing, etc)

Knitted sachet

Make two pieces as follows:
1 Cast on 18 stitches.
2 Knit 18 rows. Bind off.

3 Place two pieces together. Using contrasting yarn, work blanket stitch around three sides.
4 Fill with stuffing and potpourri.
5 Work blanket stitch along the remaining open side. Fasten off.
6 In one corner, make a loop of three strands of yarn and work buttonhole stitch around the loop.

Crochet sachet

Make two pieces as follows:

1 Chain 16.
2 Base row: 1 single crochet in 3rd chain from hook, 1 single crochet in each chain to end. Turn.
3 Pattern row: 2 chain to count as first single crochet, 1 single crochet in each stitch. Turn.
4 Repeat pattern row 15 times. Fasten off.
5 Finish as for knitted sachet, steps 3 to 5.
6 Using yarn double, make a 12-chain loop. Fasten off. Sew loop to one corner.

Paired decreasing on a right-side row

Most methods of decreasing leave a stitch that lies at an angle, which may be used as a decorative feature of the garment. Raglan armhole shaping uses pairs of decreases—one at each end of the row or side of the armhole. The first decrease follows the eventual slope of the edge to the left, while the second decrease slopes to the right. A one- two- or three-stitch border between the edge and decrease accentuates the shaping.

In this course we introduce a new method of decreasing. The decrease is made by means of a slipped stitch, and the knitting terminology for it is "slip one, knit one, pass slipped stitch over (sl1, K1, psso)". It makes a slope to the left on the right side of the work.

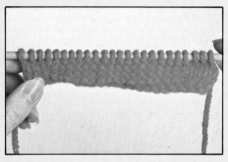

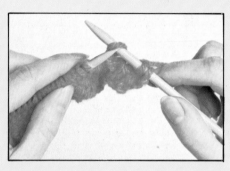

1 Here the raglan edges are emphasized by means of borders consisting of three stockinette stitches; these contrast with main fabric in reverse stockinette stitch. The decreases are made where border meets main fabric.

2 On a right-side row the first decrease needs to slope to the left. Knit the first two border stitches, then slip the next stitch knitwise.

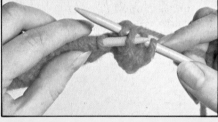

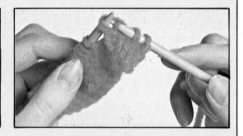

3 Knit the next stitch—even though it is part of the main fabric. As the decreasing progresses the number of stitches in the main fabric is reduced, while the 3-stitch border remains constant.

4 Insert left-hand needle from left to right through the front of the slipped stitch to begin the first decrease.

5 Slide stitches toward end of right-hand needle. Lift slipped stitch over last knitted stitch and off right-hand needle; withdraw left-hand needle. Steps 2-5 form the decrease called "slip one, knit one, pass slipped stitch over (sl1, K1, psso)".

6 Work—in this case purl—to within one stitch of the border at the other end. The decreasing must start one stitch before the border to maintain the correct number of edge stitches.

7 On a right-side row, the last decrease must slope to the right: an ordinary decrease is sufficient here. Knit the next two stitches (ie. one stitch from the main fabric and the first of the border stitches) together. Work to the end of the row.

8 This picture shows the effect of this type of decreasing worked on alternate right-side rows (ie. three rows between decreasing). The border at the beginning of the row slopes to the left and the one at the end slopes to the right.

Fred Mancini

Paired decreasing on a wrong-side row

  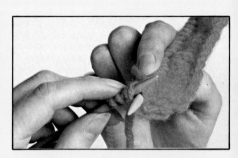

1 At the beginning of a wrong-side row you need a decrease that slopes to the right on the right side of the work: this is the opposite of how the border slopes on the wrong side. Purl the first two border stitches.

2 Purl the next two stitches (the last border stitch and the first stitch from the main fabric) together. This ordinary decrease gives the required effect on the right side.

3 Work to within one stitch of the border at the end of the row. For a border that slopes to the left on the right side of the work, purl the next two stitches together *through the back of the loops.*

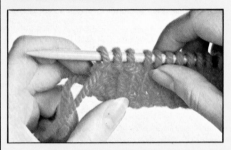  

4 Work to the end of the row. Notice that the fabric is definitely not reversible. It is quite acceptable, however, to have a stockinette stitch main fabric with a stockinette stitch border if you prefer.

5 This is how the wrong side of the work looks when you decrease on every row, alternating instructions for paired decreasings on wrong-side rows with those for decreasing on right-side rows.

6 This shows the finished effect of this type of decreasing worked on every row. The edges incline much more sharply than when you decrease on every fourth row (see step 8, page 49); for a moderately sloped edge decrease on every right-side row.

Sewing in a zipper

There are a number of occasions when you may need to fit zippers to knitted fabrics. Back neck openings (especially useful on children's sweaters for extra room when pulling them on) and skirt side or back seams need the ordinary zipper, which is closed at the bottom. Open-ended zippers are ideal for fronts of cardigans and jackets. Use the same zippers for knitting as you would for dressmaking: you may need heavier zippers in some cases, as knitted fabrics tend to be heavier than dress fabrics.

Match the length of the opening and of the zipper exactly: sewing a zipper that is too short into an opening makes the seam bulge while one that is too long will drag the sides of the opening.

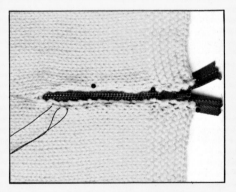 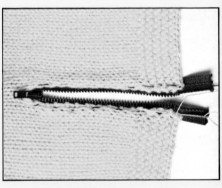

1 Working on the right side of the fabric, pin zipper into opening with teeth facing upward. Take care to match both sections of the garment exactly, and avoid stretching the knitting. Pin zipper so that the sides of the opening meet and the teeth are concealed. With thicker fabrics, such as those for outdoor wear, leave the zipper teeth exposed. Baste along both sides, using ordinary sewing thread.

2 Remove pins. Thread sewing needle to match the color of the fabric. Open the zipper carefully. Secure thread at back of top right-hand side of zipper. Bring needle through to front and back into the fabric a minute distance to the right. This is called a "stab" stitch.

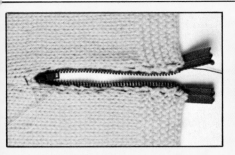

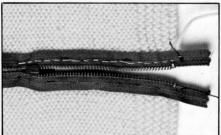

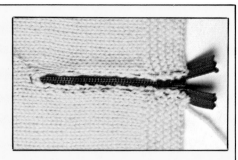

3 Bring the needle through to the front again about ¼in (5mm) to the left of the previous stitch. Repeat these stab stitches down as close as possible to the edge of the work.

4 The stitches are invisible on the right side of the knitting, as the fine thread sinks down into the thicker yarn. On the back of the zipper are the longer strands between the stitches.

5 For a back neck or skirt side seam opening, work a few extra stitches across bottom of zipper before continuing up the other side; work the second side separately (easier with zipper closed).

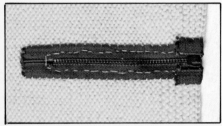

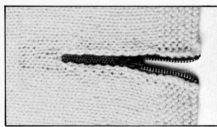

6 To finish off the wrong side of the work, fold the extended tapes back so that the fold is level with the top of the zipper: angle them slightly to the side to avoid obstructing zipper slide. Pin in position. If zipper is being inserted into neckband that folds to the inside, the top of zipper itself will reach only to the fold line and the tapes will be enclosed between the layers.

7 Neaten the tapes and keep them in position by overcasting all around outer edges; this is normally done with matching thread. Sew down the folded-back tapes at the top in the same way.

8 The finished zipper must open easily on the right side of the work without the opening slide catching any knitted edge; if this does happen then you have stitched too close to the teeth of the zipper.

Warm for winter

Here's a bathrobe any child will warm to—a snug, soft-colored robe with a jolly, pixie-style hood. It's easy to knit, in reverse stockinette stitch, and fastens with a zipper.

Sizes
To fit 20[22:24]in (51[56:61]cm) chest.
Length, 29[32:34]in (73[80:87]cm).
Sleeve seam, 8[9:10]in (20[23:26]cm).

Note Directions for larger sizes are in brackets []: where there is only one set of figures it applies to all sizes.

Materials
23[27:29]oz (650[750:800]g) of a
  bulky novelty yarn
1 pair each Nos. 7 and 9 (5mm and
  6mm) knitting needles
18[20:22]in (46[51:56]cm) open-
  ended zipper

Gauge
13 sts and 19 rows to 4in (10cm) in stockinette st on No. 9 (6mm) needles.

Back
Using No. 9 (6mm) needles cast on 67[73:79] sts.
1st row K1, (P1, K1) to end.
2nd row P1, (K1, P1) to end.
Rep these 2 rows twice. Beg with P row, cont in reverse stockinette st, work 16 rows. Dec one st at each end of next and every foll 6th row until 37[41:45] sts rem. Cont without shaping until work measures 24[26:28]in (61[66:71]cm) from beg, ending with a K row.
Shape raglan armholes
**Bind off 2 sts at beg of next 2 rows.
Next row K3, P to last 3 sts, K3.
Next row P3, K to last 3 sts, P3.
Next row K2, sl1, K1, psso, P to last 4 sts, K2tog, K2.
Keeping 3 sts at each end in stockinette st throughout cont to dec in same way

on every foll 4th row 1[2:3] times more, then on every other row until 13[15:17] sts rem, ending with a WS row. **Bind off.

Left front
Using No. 9 (6mm) needles cast on

35[37:41] sts.
1st row (K1, P1) to last 3 sts, K3.
2nd row K2, P1, (K1, P1) to end.
Rep the last 2 rows twice more but inc one st at end of last row on 2nd size only. 35[38:41] sts.
Next row P to last 2 sts, K2.
Next row K to end.
Rep last 2 rows 7 times more.
Keeping 2 sts at front edge in garter st, dec one st at beg of next and every foll 6th row until 20[22:24] sts rem. Cont without shaping until work measures same as back to armholes, ending with WS row.

Shape raglan armhole
Bind off 2 sts at beg of next row.
Work 1 row.
Next row K3, P to last 2 sts, K2.
Next row K to last 3 sts, P3.
Next row K2, sl1, K1, psso, P to last 2 sts, K2.
Dec at beg of every 4th row 1[2:3] times more, then at beg of every other row until 14[15:16] sts rem, ending with a RS row.

Shape neck
Next row Bind off 2[3:4] sts, K to last 3 sts, P3.
Next row K2, sl1, K1, psso, P to last 2 sts, P2tog.
Next row K to last 3 sts, P3.
Rep the last 2 rows 3 times more. 4 sts.

Next row K2, sl1, K1, psso.
Next row P3.
Next row K1, sl1, K1, psso.
Next row P2tog. Fasten off.

Right front
Using No. 9 (6mm) needles cast on 35[37:41] sts.
1st row K3, (P1, K1) to end.
2nd row (P1, K1) to last 3 sts, P1, K2.
Rep the last 2 rows twice more but inc one st at beg of last row on 2nd size only. 35[38:41] sts.
Next row K2, P to end.
Next row K to end.
Work to match left front, reversing shaping.

Sleeves
Using No. 7 (5mm) needles cast on 21[23:25] sts. and rib 6 rows as for back. Change to No. 9 (6mm) needles and beg with P row, cont in reverse stockinette st inc one st at each end of first and every foll 8th row until there are 29[33:37] sts. Cont without shaping until sleeve measures 8[9:10]in (20[23:26]cm) from beg, ending with a K row.

Shape raglan armhole
Rep from ** to ** of back, but dec until 7 sts rem, ending with a WS row.
Next row K2, sl 1, K2 tog, psso, K2.

Next row P5. Bind off.

Hood
Using No. 7 (5mm) needles cast on 53[57:61] sts and rib 6 rows as back. Change to No. 9 (6mm) needles and beg with P row cont in reverse stockinette st until work measures 5½[6¼:7]in (14[16:18]cm) from beg, ending with a K row and dec one st at center of last row. 52[56:60] sts.

Shape back
Next row P1, *P2tog, P10[11:12], rep from * 3 times more, P2tog, P1. 47[51:55] sts. Work 3 rows.
Next row P1, *P2tog, P9[10:11], rep from * twice more, P2tog, P8[9:10], P2tog, P1. 42[46:50] sts.
Cont to dec in this way, working one st less between each decrease on every 4th row until 12[11:10] sts rem. Cut off yarn, thread through sts, draw up and fasten off.

To finish
Press work lightly with a cool iron over a dry cloth. Join raglan seams. Join side and sleeve seams. Sew hood to neck edge then join rem part of hood seam. Sew in zipper placing the top at neck edge and leaving bottom part of front edge free. Make a tassel and sew to end of hood. Press seams.

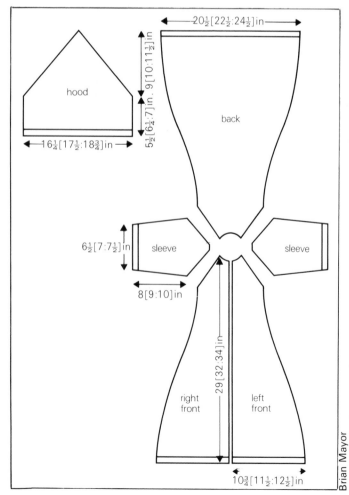

Brian Mayor

S. Wells

52

Sewing/COURSE 15

*Staystitching
*Facings
*Buttonholes—handmade
*Buttonholes—machine-made
*A short-sleeved jacket:
  directions for making (2)

Staystitching

Staystitching is used to reinforce a weak point in the construction of a garment such as a slashed corner, or to help retain the shape at a seamline cut on the bias, which would stretch out of shape when handled. Any staystitching must be done immediately after cutting out and before any other sewing is begun.

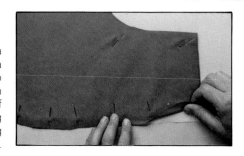

1 If you are working on a very slippery or stretchy fabric, cut out an extra pattern piece in firm paper and pin and baste the garment piece to it. Then staystitch through both fabric and paper.

2 To staystitch, stitch one row of straight machine stitching close to the seamline on the seam allowance. Do not stretch fabric while stitching. After stitching, carefully tear away the paper without stretching fabric. On non-slippery fabric, do not use paper.

Facings

A facing is used on a garment for one or more purposes: to provide a neat finish, to conceal a raw edge, or to maintain the shape of a neckline, an armhole, a front or back opening, a collar or cuffs. The facing can either be cut in one piece with the garment section or cut and applied separately, as it is on the jacket featured in this course.

A separate facing is usually cut on the same grain as the edge it is to finish. On a curved edge, such as a rounded neckline, the facing is cut on the same curved grain as the neckline edge of the garment. Some patterns include a separate piece for a facing; others indicate that a facing should be cut by means of a cutting line marked on the main pattern piece. Where a facing is used, it is usually strengthened by an interfacing, which is cut either from the facing pattern piece or from a separate piece.

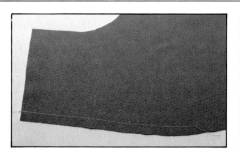

1 Stitch a row of staystitching on the neck edge of both garment sections $\frac{1}{8}$in (3mm) away from the seam line on the seam allowance.

2 Baste interfacing sections to wrong side of garment sections and catchstitch inner, unnotched edge to garment. Join front to back at side and shoulder seams. Press seams open and finish raw edges.

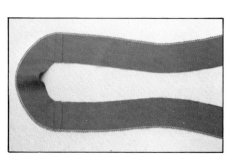

3 With right sides together and notches matching, baste and stitch the front and back neck facings together at the shoulder seams. Finish and press seams open. Finish the inner, unnotched edge of facing, stitch $\frac{1}{4}$in (6mm) from edge trim to $\frac{1}{8}$in (3mm) and overcast.

4 With right sides together and notches and shoulder seams matching, pin and baste the facings to the front edge and front and back neck edge. Stitch around entire facing.

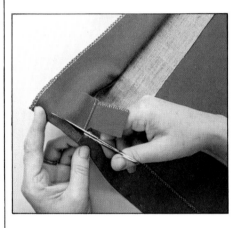

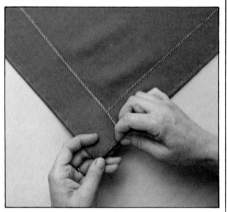

Paul Williams

5 Grade the seam allowances trimming interfacing close to stitching line. Press the seam allowances toward the facing. If you are not going to topstitch the edge, understitch the facing to the seam allowance.

6 Turn the facing to the wrong side, and with the right side of the garment uppermost baste close to the stitched edge. Catchstitch facing to shoulder seam allowance. Trim the excess interfacing even with the hem foldline.

7 When the facing reaches to the hemline of an opening, as on a jacket, a coat, and sometimes on a dress, the hem must be turned up before the facing is turned in at the hemline and finished. Release the basting at the hem edge of the facing for about 4in (10cm). Turn the facing outward and turn the hem up the required amount. Then sew the hem.

8 If the fabric is bulky, you can trim away the excess fabric of the hemline of the facing and from the hem allowance under the facing. Trim the facing to $\frac{3}{8}$in (1cm) and the hem allowance to $\frac{5}{8}$in (1.5cm) at the hemline.

9 Sew the remaining hem in position. Press foldline of hem flat.

10 Turn facing to the inside, baste front edge again and slipstitch lower folded edges together. Then hem inner edge of facing to hem allowance, using very small hand stitches.

Buttonholes

It is a shame to spoil a well-made garment with badly made buttonholes. Making a buttonhole is not really difficult, and doing it well is very satisfying. Remember that practice makes perfect. Before making the buttonholes on any garment, make a practice buttonhole on a piece of the fabric you are using, including facing and interfacing, if any. Handmade buttonholes are cut before they are sewed and for this you need a pair of buttonhole scissors. These have a screw to set the required length of the buttonhole. Always test the length before cutting the garment. The size and spacing of the buttonholes are indicated on the pattern piece, but you may have to make

alterations if you use a button which is a different size from that recommended in the directions. Spacing may also be affected if you alter the size of the piece in which you are placing the buttonholes.
If you use a larger button you may need fewer buttonholes. If you change the size of the buttons check the distance between the center front of the garment and the finished edge. The extension should be one half the diameter of the button, plus $\frac{1}{4}$in (6mm) to $\frac{5}{8}$in (1.5cm). Increase or decrease the width of the extension accordingly if the button size is changed.
Buttonholes must be at least $\frac{1}{8}$in (3mm) longer than the diameter of the button. If

the button is thick, the buttonhole must be even larger. The general rule is that the hole must be at least the diameter of the button plus its depth. Making a practice buttonhole will show you how much extra length is required.
Handmade or machine-made buttonholes are made after the garment is complete, whereas bound buttonholes (to be explained in a future volume) have to be made during the construction of the garment. The type of buttonhole to be used on the garment is usually indicated in the pattern instructions. The spacing and positions of the buttonholes and button placings are generally marked on the pattern.

Handmade buttonholes

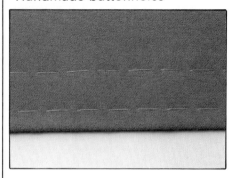

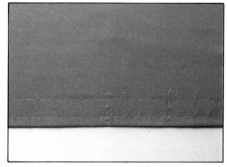

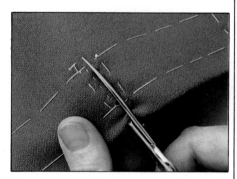

1 Handmade buttonholes must be cut exactly on the grain of the fabric. Mark horizontal buttonholes on the crosswise grain and vertical ones on the lengthwise grain. Transfer buttonhole markings from the pattern to the wrong side of the garment, then baste through the fabric so the markings appear on the right side. Mark the length with a row of vertical basting at each end.

2 Mark cutting line at each hole with basting between these two rows.

3 After marking the buttonholes, work a row of basting stitches close to the cutting line on both sides. This will hold the fabric layers together when making the buttonhole stitches. Using matching thread, sew a row of small running stitches $\frac{1}{8}$in (3mm) on each side of the buttonhole cutting line. Using a pair of buttonhole scissors adjusted to the required length, cut along marking.

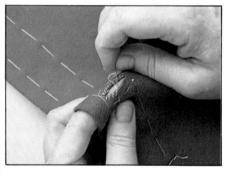

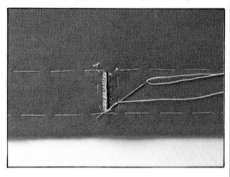

4 Using synthetic or cotton thread, sew a row of overcasting stitches around the buttonhole edge to prevent raveling while you work.

5 Thread a fine needle with a single piece of thread, about 30-35in (80-90cm) long. Secure the thread on the wrong side with a double backstitch at the lower left-hand inner end of the buttonhole.

6 Bring the needle to the right side and sew buttonhole stitch (Sewing Course 8, Volume 2, page 45) along the lower edge of the buttonhole. Make the stitches close and even, and deep enough to cover the overcasting stitches.

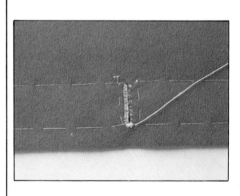

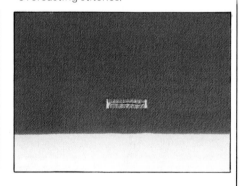

7 When you reach the right-hand outer end of the buttonhole change to overcasting stitch, fanning the stitches around the end. Then continue in buttonhole stitch until you reach the inner end.

8 At the inner end make several stitches across the width of the buttonhole stitching to make a bar tack. Make the stitches through fabric and over the threads of the existing stitches.

9 Vertical buttonholes are made in the same way as horizontal buttonholes, except that both ends are finished with a bar tack. They are used where you have a narrow placket—on a loose fitting garment such as a shirt or blouse. They should not be used where they will get any strain or the garment will gape.

Machine-made buttonholes

Making buttonholes by machine saves time and gives good results on most fabrics. Here again, it is essential to work a test buttonhole on the actual fabric you are using. Automatic machines make buttonholes without an attachment, but for the standard machine a special buttonhole attachment is required.

Mark the buttonhole positions as described for handmade buttonholes and then follow the directions given in the machine manual for making buttonholes.

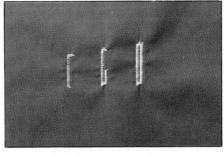

1 The machine will first stitch a bar across the width of the buttonhole, then one side of the buttonhole working toward you. Then a bar at the end of the buttonhole and reverse stitch along the remaining edge.

2 Using a seam ripper, insert the point of the ripper in the center of the buttonhole as close to the bar stitching as possible and cut between the stitching to the center of the buttonhole. Cut the other end of the buttonhole in the same way. Do not be tempted to cut the buttonhole in one continuous movement as it is easy to make a slip.

Paul Williams

A short-sleeved jacket: directions for making (2)

The following directions are for completing the short-sleeved jacket begun in the previous course, Volume 3, page 69.

Facings

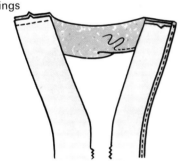

1 With right sides together and notches matching, join the front and back neck facings together at the shoulder seams. Press seams open. Finish the outer edge of the facings by turning in $\frac{1}{4}$in (6mm) and stitching. Press stitched edge flat.

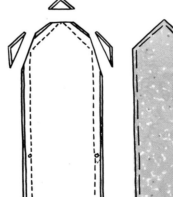

2 Staystitch the front neck of the jacket to prevent stretching. Apply the facings to the jacket front and neck edges as instructed in this course, but do not understitch. Grade the seam allowances, turn facing to inside and baste close to stitched edge. Press.

2 Next, trim the interfacing close to stitching. Grade seam allowances and cut across corners. Turn tab right side out and baste around edges. Press.

Tabs and buttonholes

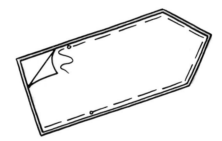

1 Baste interfacing to wrong side of one tab section. With right sides together and outer edges matching, baste both tab pieces together, leaving the lower edges open. Stitch seam.

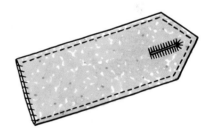

3 Close the lower edges by hand overcasting. Topstitch around tab, $\frac{1}{4}$in (6mm) in from outer edges. Press flat on wrong side. Repeat for other tabs. Mark and sew hand or machine buttonholes in positions indicated.

Pockets

1 Finish the top edge of the pocket facing by turning in $\frac{1}{4}$in (6mm) and machine stitching. Fold pocket facing over right side of pocket along fold line. Baste and stitch ends. Cut across corners.

2 Turn pocket right side out. Turn in the seam allowance around the side and lower edges and baste around all edges of pocket. Press pocket flat on wrong side. With the wrong side of the tab placed to the wrong side of the pocket, baste tab to inside edge between circles.

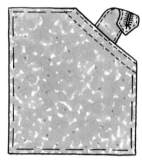

3 On the right side, topstitch $\frac{1}{4}$in (6mm) in from the edge and then stitch a second row of topstitching a further $\frac{3}{4}$in (2cm) in, securing the tab when doing so. Repeat for second pocket.

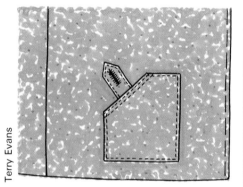

4 Baste pockets to jacket fronts in position indicated on pattern. Topstitch pockets in place, stitching $\frac{1}{4}$in (6mm) in from side, bottom and top edge of pockets. Press flat on the wrong side.

Terry Evans

pattern pack

Caroline Arber

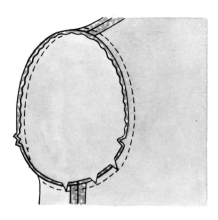

front facing to the inside and slipstitch edges to hem—without stitching through to right side.

Topstitching and buttons

Terry Evans

Sleeves

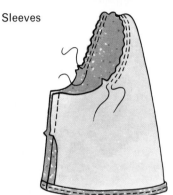

1 Add two rows of ease-stitching around the sleeve cap between notches. With right sides together and notches matching, baste and stitch the underarm seam of sleeve. Finish and press seam open. Turn in lower edge by $\frac{1}{4}$in (6mm) and stitch. Press.

3 With right sides together and matching notches, underarm seams and circle to shoulder seam, pin sleeve into armhole, pulling up gathering threads to ease in fullness. Baste, spreading ease evenly. Stitch seam, placing sleeve uppermost. Press seam allowance towards sleeve. Clip curves.

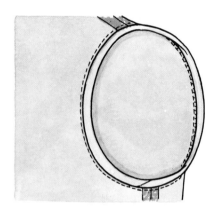

4 Trim seam allowance to $\frac{1}{4}$in (6mm) and finish the raw edges together with purchased bias binding.

1 Stitch a row of topstitching $\frac{1}{4}$in (6mm) in from front and neck edges and another row a further $\frac{3}{4}$in (2cm) in. Add a row of topstitching around armhole $\frac{1}{4}$in (6mm) from armhole seam line. Sew buttons to sleeve and pockets

2 Turn sleeve hem up along fold line and baste close to folded edge. Sew hem to sleeve using hemming stitch. Press folded edge only. Baste tab to inside of sleeve at lower edge between circles. On the right side topstitch $\frac{1}{4}$in (6mm) in from lower edge. Add a second row of stitching a further $\frac{3}{4}$in (2cm) in, securing tab when doing so. Repeat steps 1 and 2 for second sleeve.

Hem

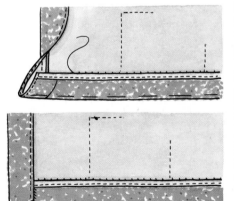

1 Turn front facing out. Turn hem up and baste close to folded edge. Finish raw edge of hem and sew to jacket using the straight binding method (see Sewing Course 13, Volume 3, page 63). Turn the

Working with jersey material

Jersey is a popular material in the fashion world since it is relatively easy to work with and comfortable to wear. It appears in every type of garment from casual sportswear to evening dress. It is now available in a great variety of weights and fibers. There are interesting prints as well as multicolor patterns knitted directly into the fabric. The textures range from fine and silky to rough and bulky fabrics resembling hand knits. Even lacy patterns are available in jersey. Jersey fabric requires some special methods in both cutting out and sewing. A special ballpoint needle, which is designed especially for sewing knitted and synthetic fabrics, must be used. If you use an ordinary needle, stitches may be missed and loops may form on the reverse side of the work, or you may find the machine does not stitch at all. The needle can also split the threads of the fabric and cause runs. The seams need no finishing as jersey does not ravel.

Jersey will drop slightly, so allow the garment to hang on a hanger for a day or two before turning up the hem.

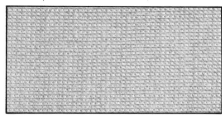

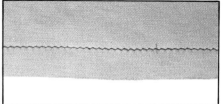

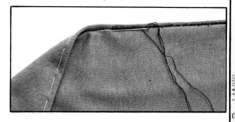

1 For cutting, lay the material so it is completely flat and not stretched in any way. The lengthwise rib in jersey is comparable to the lengthwise thread of a woven fabric and it is used as a guide for placing pattern pieces on the straight grain. Place each pattern piece so that the lengthwise grain marking on the pattern is parallel to a lengthwise rib. Some jersey fabrics have a slight nap or texture; if so, place all pattern pieces in the same direction. After removing the pattern, staystitch all bias and curved seamlines.

2 Use an automatic stretch stitch if your machine has one, or a very small zig-zag stitch, as this stitch will stretch when the seam is stretched. If your machine does not do either of these stitches, use a slightly shorter than average straight stitch but stretch the seam slightly when stitching it. This gives added elasticity and helps prevent the stitches from breaking and the seams from pulling when the garment is worn. Reinforce crosswise seams with a narrow ribbon or straight seam binding (see "Stay tape" page 61).

3 Sew hems invisibly with catch-stitch or with herringbone stitch (see page 61). Like other materials, jersey should be pressed during the process of construction.

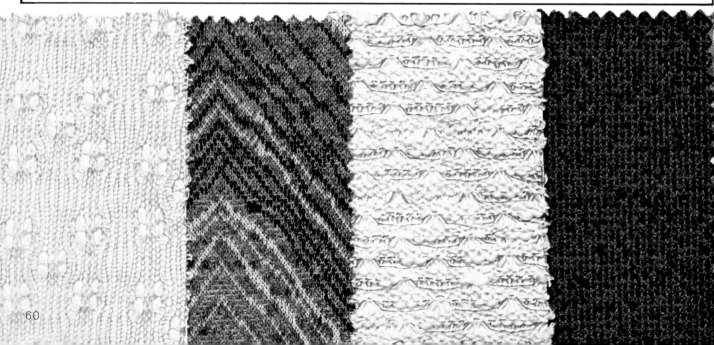

Stay tape

A stay tape is a method used to reinforce a weak area in the construction of a garment. It is used in the same places as stay stitching but gives a stronger support. It is also used in a wide variety of places where stay stitching cannot be used, such as at a waist seamline where both the skirt and the bodice are gathered, or where an area is to be gathered and there is no seam. Straight seam binding or ribbon $\frac{1}{2}$in (1.2cm) wide can be used as stay tape. On a neck or armhole where there is a deep curve, use a $\frac{1}{8}$in (3mm)- to $\frac{1}{4}$in (6mm)-wide ribbon.

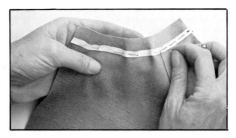

1 With the wrong side of the garment section uppermost, place the binding centrally over the seamline. Pin and baste in place, being careful not to stretch the garment fabric out of shape while doing so.

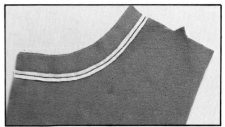

2 Stitch the seam in the normal way. The line of stitching should run down the center of the binding.

Herringbone stitch

Herringbone stitch is more widely known as an embroidery stitch but is also used in dressmaking. It is particularly useful on jersey fabrics as a method of hemming, because of the stretchy quality of the stitch.

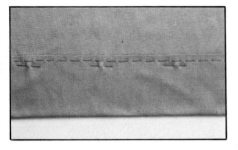

1 Turn up, baste and trim the hem allowance to the required depth. The stitch is sewed from left to right. Begin by working a double back stitch on the wrong side, upper edge, of the hem allowance.

2 Bring the needle to the right side of the hem allowance. Hold the needle so that it is pointing to the left. Take the needle up and slightly to the right and pick up a couple of threads of the garment fabric, even with the top of the hem allowance. These stitches should not show on right side of garment.

3 Take the needle down and slightly to the right and pick up a couple of threads about $\frac{1}{8}$in (3mm) to the right, through the edge of the hem allowance only. Continue along the hem. The spacing will depend on the thickness of the fabric. On fine wool, for example, make the stitches $\frac{1}{8}$in (3mm) apart.

This selection of jersey shows the great variety of types available, made from both natural and synthetic fibers.

Paul Williams

Ray Duns

*Fitting problems on a garment with an open neckline
*Applying an all-in-one neck and armhole facing
*T-shirt top: directions for making

Fitting problems on a garment with an open neckline

Gaping neckline

An open neckline can give a very flattering look to a simple top—whether for evening wear or beachwear. However, the effect is lost if the opening does not lie neatly in place. If your figure deviates from the standard pattern measurements, it is worth making a muslin shell before cutting out the actual garment, and adjusting the pattern to your own figure. If an open neckline is too big it gapes or falls away from the body. The excess fabric must be taken out of the neckline so it will lie smoothly. Make any alterations to the shell and then transfer the alterations to the pattern before cutting out in fabric. The T-shirt pattern used in this course is cut for stretch fabrics only, and so there is no ease allowance in it. Cut out the shell from the two main pattern pieces, adding an opening at the center back (plus seam allowance), so that it is easy to slip on and off for fitting.

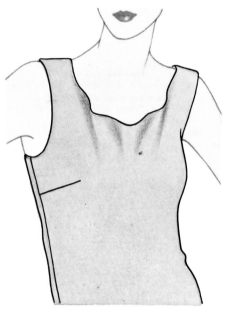

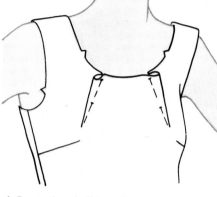

1 Baste the shell together and try it on. Take in the necessary amount by pinning at each side of the neckline. If the amount to be taken in is more than ½in (1.2cm) make more than one tuck at each side. Mark the tucks and remove the pins.

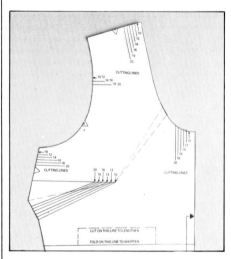

2 Transfer the markings to the pattern and draw the tuck lines from the neckline to the point of the bust dart.

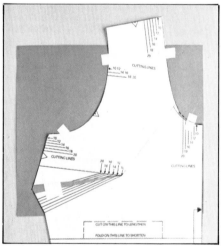

3 Slash along the center of the tuck to the point; also slash along the center of the bust dart from the side seam almost to the point, but do not cut through. Lap the pattern at the neckline so that the tuck lines match, and tape in place. This will open the bust dart. Place a sheet of paper under the pattern. Redraw the neck curve. When stitching the bust dart, follow the original stitching lines to take in the extra fullness produced.

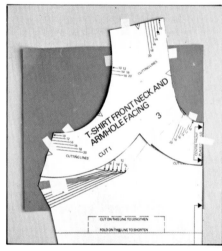

4 The same alteration must be made to the neck facing. Slash the facing and take out the same amount at the neckline. Redraw the cutting line at the neck edge.
Check that the facing pattern has been altered to the correct shape by laying it over the bodice neckline. They should match.

Gaping armhole

If the armhole gapes there is too much length in the garment from the shoulder to the underarm and a fold will form at the underarm. This fullness must be taken out at the armhole, and here again it is necessary to make a muslin shell in order to make the alteration.

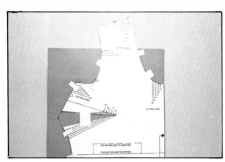

1 Take in the necessary amount on the shell at the armhole by pinning. If the amount is less than $\frac{1}{2}$in (1.2cm), adjust the pattern by making a tuck in the armhole curve. Taper the tuck so that the pattern will lie flat. Tape in place over a piece of paper, and redraw the cutting line at the armhole. Make the same alteration to the armhole facing. Check the new shape on the facing against the bodice.

2 If the adjustment is more than $\frac{1}{2}$in (1.2cm), draw tuck lines from the armhole to the point of the bust dart. Slash along the center of tuck and dart. Lap pattern for tuck and tape in place. The bust dart will open. Tape some paper under the dart and redraw the cutting lines. Make the same alteration to the facing. When stitching the bust dart, follow the original stitching lines to take in the excess fullness produced.

Applying an all-in-one neck and armhole facing

This is often used on garments with narrow shoulders, such as T-shirts and dresses which are both collarless and sleeveless—the shoulder width being too narrow to take separate facings at both neck and armhole. The facing is applied to the neck and armhole after the side seams are joined, but before the shoulder seams of facing and garment are stitched.

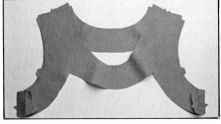

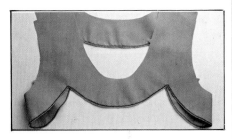

1 Staystitch or stay tape the neck and armhole edges. Before applying the facing to the garment, pin a very small tuck in the center of both the front and back shoulders of the garment only as shown. This will ensure that the facing or seams will not show on right side.

2 Baste and stitch the front and back facings together at the side seams with right sides together and notches matching. Press seams open.

3 Finish the outer edge of the facing by the method most suited to your fabric. Jersey fabrics may be finished with zig-zag machine stitching.

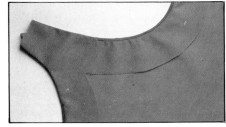

4 Pin and baste the front and back neck and armhole facing to the garment with right sides together and notches matching around the neck and armhole edges. Stitch seams to within $\frac{5}{8}$in (1.5cm) of the shoulder edges. Secure the thread ends firmly and grade the seam allowance and notch the curves.

5 Remove the pins and release the tuck in the shoulders of the garment. Turn the facing to the inside.

6 If the garment is not to be top-stitched, understitch the facing to the seam allowance close to the seamlines to prevent the facing rolling to the right side of the garment. Begin and end the stitching about $2\frac{3}{4}$in (7cm) from the shoulder line. Hem the facing to the side seam allowance only.

continued

Paul Williams

7 At the shoulders, fold the facing seam allowance back and pin out of the way of the seamline. Baste and stitch the shoulder seams of the garment with right sides together and notches matching. Trim seams and press open.

8 Turn in the facing seam allowances and slip stitch the facings together over the garment shoulder seams.

9 Baste around the neck and armhole edges with the right side of the garment uppermost, easing into a good shape while doing so. Press stitched edges flat on the wrong side. Press shoulder seams flat. Add topstitching, if required, around neck and armhole.

T-shirt: directions for making

This is a simple T-shirt pattern designed for stretch fabrics. Try it in colorful cotton or synthetic jersey for a summer top, or make it in something "glittery" for parties. This top is ideal for summer picnics, but equally successful at winter parties.

Measurements
The pattern is given in sizes 10, 12, 14, 16, 18 and 20, corresponding to sizes 8–18 in ready-made clothes. A guide to our sizes is on page 2.

Finished length 28in (71cm).

Suggested fabrics
This pattern is suitable only for stretch fabrics such as cotton or synthetic jersey and stretch terry cloth.

Materials
36in (90cm) or 45in (115cm)-wide fabric with or without nap:
Sizes 10, 12, 14: $2\frac{3}{8}$yd (2.10m)
Sizes 16, 18, 20: $2\frac{1}{2}$yd (2.20m)
54in (140cm)-wide fabric with or without nap:
Sizes 10, 12, $1\frac{1}{4}$yd (1.10m)
Sizes 14, 16, 18, 20: $1\frac{3}{8}$yd (1.20m)
Matching sewing thread

cutting layout

54in-wide fabric with or without nap

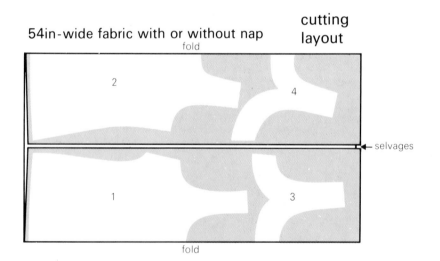

36in and 45in-wide fabric with or without nap

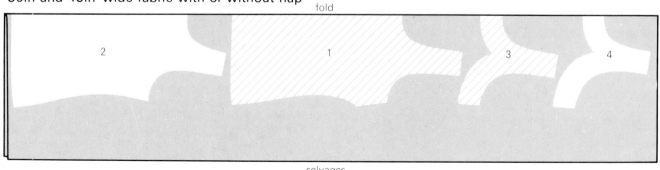

Key to pattern pieces

1 T-shirt front   Cut 1 on fold
2 T-shirt back   Cut 1 on fold
3 Front neck and   Cut 1 on fold
   armhole facing
4 Back neck and   Cut 1 on fold
   armhole facing

Cutting out

1 Cut out the pattern pieces from the pattern sheet following the correct line for the size you want.
2 Prepare the fabric and pin on the pattern pieces, following the layouts provided here. Make sure you place the pieces with the direction line along the ribs of the fabric (if using jersey). Cut out the fabric, following closely the edge of the pattern piece.
3 Transfer all pattern markings.

Assembling

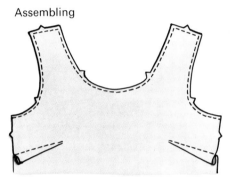

1 Stay stitch the neck and armhole edges. (If using a very stretchy fabirc, use stay tape instead.)
Pin, baste and stitch the bust darts, with right sides together. Press darts down toward hem.

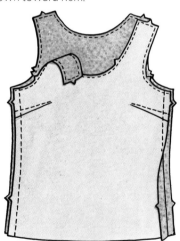

2 Baste the shoulder and side seams, right sides together, matching notches. Try on the T-shirt and make any necessary alterations by pinning. Then, if necessary, re-baste the side seams. Unpick the shoulder seam basting and mark the shoulder seam line on both front and back shoulders with a line of basting. Stitch the side seams only. Press seams open.

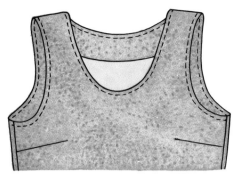

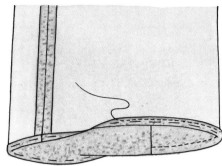

3 Apply the all-in-one facing to the neck and armhole edges as shown on page 63, omitting the understitching. Baste close to the stitched edges and press flat. Topstitch around the neck and armhole edges ¼in (6mm) in from the outer edge. Press and remove basting.

4 At the lower edge of the T-shirt, turn up ¼in (6mm) and then a further ⅜in (1cm) and baste. Machine stitch $\frac{5}{16}$in (8mm) in from the lower hem edge. Press hem flat.

Serge Krouglikoff

pattern pack

Sewing/COURSE 18

*More fitting problems
*Open-ended darts
*Slot zipper
  application
*Dress: directions
  for making (1)

Normally you choose a pattern size according to your bust measurement. For example, if your bust size is 34in (87cm), you should use a size 12 pattern—even if your waist and hips do not correspond to the measurements for that pattern size. The reason for this is that it is easier to adjust waist and hip measurements than to adjust the bust measurement.

In some cases, however, it may still be necessary to adjust the bustline of the pattern. In a previous course we explained how to alter the pattern for a high or low bustline. Alteration may also be necessary if the bust itself is large or small in relation to the overall measurement: for example, if you have a narrow back, but a full bosom (say a C cup), the overall measurement may be deceptively small, and the pattern will need increasing across the front.

Large bust

A large bust will cause wrinkles and pulling across the bust area of a garment. Therefore, more fullness must be allowed in the pattern.

To determine how much extra fullness is required over the bust area, measure over the fullest part of the bust from side seam to side seam and add 1in (2.5cm) to this measurement. Then measure pattern in the same place. The difference in the measurement will be the amount of adjustment.

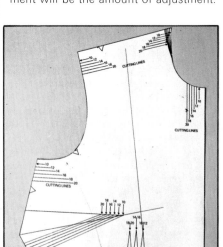

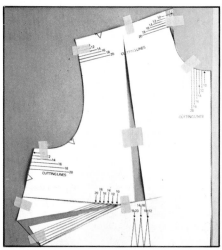

1 To find the bust point on the pattern, draw a line through the center of the bust dart to the center front and from the center of the shoulder seamline to the point of the waist dart. These lines will cross at the bust point. Remember to adjust the pattern to your own bust point level if necessary (see Sewing Course 14, Volume 3, page 66).

2 Slash the pattern horizontally along the center of the bust dart to the bust point. Slash the upper bodice from the bust point to the shoulder seamline (not to the cutting line). At the bust point, spread the horizontal slash by half the required amount of adjustment. Insert paper behind the slashes and tape in place. Shorten the bust dart by 1in (2.5cm). Redraw new dart lines from original points at side edges to new dart point. Fold the dart and cut on the new cutting line at the side edge for the new dart shape.

Small bust

A small bust will cause wrinkles to fall across the bust area of the garment. Measure across the bust (see "Large bust"), add 1in (2.5cm) and subtract this figure from the pattern measurement. Find the bust point on the pattern (step 1 "Large bust") and proceed as shown below.

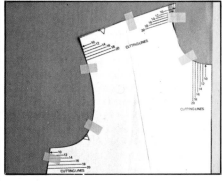

1 Slash the pattern horizontally along the center of the bust dart to the bust point. Slash upper bodice section from the bust point to the shoulder seamline (not to the cutting line). Lap the vertical slash and the bust dart by half the amount of adjustment and tape in place. The dart has now been decreased. The new dart point will be where the stitching lines intersect. Fold the dart and cut the new lines at the side edge for the new dart shape.

Hollow chest

A hollow chest will cause wrinkles in the fabric between the neckline and bust. The pattern requires less fullness in this area. Therefore, the pattern must be shortened between the neckline and the bust.

To determine how much adjustment is required, you can either work directly on the front pattern piece or cut this piece in muslin and make the adjustments on that. In either case, first pin the darts, then place the pattern or the muslin piece next to the body. Make a horizontal tuck, taking up the excess fabric or paper across the chest. This amount will be the amount of adjustment required.

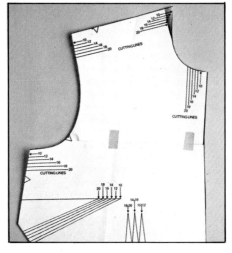

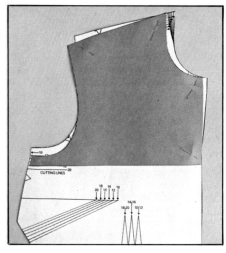

1 On a sheet of paper trace the outline of the original shape of the pattern at the center front, neckline, shoulder and armhole edges. Draw a horizontal line across the tracing just below the armhole. Lay this aside for the moment. Slash the pattern horizontally from the center front 4in (10cm) below the neckline edge to the armhole seamline. Overlap the slash at the center front by the amount of adjustment required. Tape the edges in place.

2 Pin the tracing of the front pattern over the adjusted pattern, with the center fronts aligned below the slash. Trim the altered pattern where it extends beyond the tracing of the original (on top). Then tape the two pieces to another sheet of paper and trace the whole outline onto it. The resulting pattern will contain the adjustments for the hollow chest while retaining the original lines of the shoulder, neckline and armhole.

Open ended darts

This form of dart is often referred to as a release dart, because fullness is released at the wider end. It is used in places where the designer of the garment wants an effect similar to that produced by an unpressed pleat.

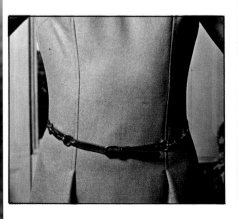

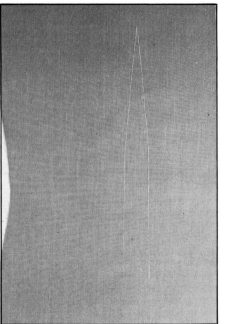

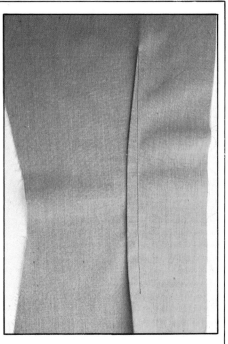

1 If the dart lines are curved, mark the stitching lines on the wrong side of the garment. If they are straight you can simply mark the darts with tailor's tacks at intervals.

2 Fold the dart, right sides together, matching stitching lines. Pin and baste the dart. Stitch the dart, starting at the open end, and using reverse stitching to secure the ends. Taper the stitching to a point and take a few stitches as close to the folded edge as possible. Finish off the thread ends securely. Press the dart toward the side seam.

Paul Williams

Slot zipper application

This type of zipper application is usually used in a center front or center back seam at the neckline of a dress or blouse or in a sleeve seam at the wrist. Insert a neck zipper before joining the side seams of the garment, since it is easier to work on a flat section than on a partially assembled garment.

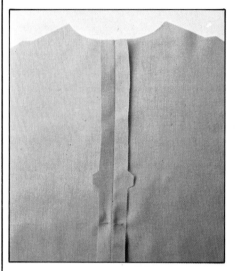

1 Turn the garment wrong side out. Pin the center back seam together at the zipper opening with right sides together and notches matching. Using the largest stitch on the machine, stitch the seam to close the opening. This will ensure that when the zipper is stitched into place both sides of the seam are even. Press the seam open. Mark the end of the opening with a pin.

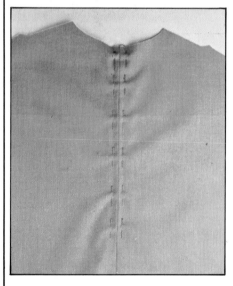

2 Working with the garment right side up, pin the zipper to the wrong side of the seam, with the seamline over the center of the teeth. Place top of zipper $\frac{1}{4}$in (6mm) below neck seamline.

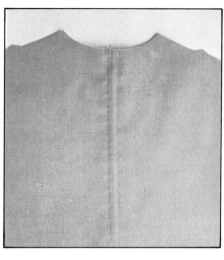

3 Baste the zipper in place, basting $\frac{1}{4}$in (6mm) to each side of the center seam.

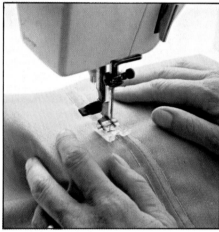

4 Using the zipper foot on the machine, stitch the zipper in place on the right side of the garment. Stitch down the left-hand side, across the bottom and up the other side.

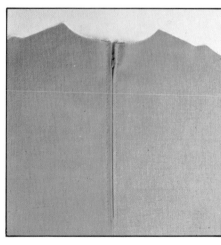

5 If you prefer, sew the zipper in by hand using tiny backstitches Romove both machine- and hand-basting. Press lightly on the wrong side.

Dress: directions for making (1)

This is the kind of comfortable, go-everywhere dress that every woman likes to have in her wardrobe. Its simple lines make it ideal for all sorts of occasions, from a shopping trip to a dinner date. The pattern for the dress is taken from the Pattern Pack. Here we give directions for beginning the basic dress. Directions for completing it are given on page 74.

Measurements
The pattern is given in sizes 10, 12, 14, 16, 18 and 20, corresponding to sizes 8-18 in ready-made clothes. A guide to our sizes is on page 2.

Suggested fabrics
Jersey knits, synthetics, wool crepe, silk, wool blends, cotton blends and linens.

Materials
45in (115cm)-wide fabric with or without nap:
Sizes 10 and 12: 3¾yd (3.5m)
Sizes 14 and 16: 3⅞yd (3.5m)
Sizes 18 and 20: 4yd (3.6m)
54in (140cm)-wide fabric without nap:
Sizes 10 and 12: 2⅜yd (2.1m)
Sizes 14 and 16: 2¼yd (2.3m)
Sizes 18 and 20: 2½yd (2.4m)
36in (90cm)-wide interfacing for all sizes: 8in (20cm)
Matching thread
22in (55cm) dress zipper
Hook and eye

Key to pattern pieces
1 Dress front   Cut 1 on fold
2 Dress back   Cut 2
3 Sleeve   Cut 2
4 Front neck facing   Cut 1 on fold
5 Back neck facing   Cut 2

Cutting out
1 Cut out the pattern pieces from the pattern sheet following the correct line for the size you want. Make any necessary adjustments to the pattern.
2 Prepare the fabric and pin on the pattern pieces, following the layouts provided. Make sure you place the pieces with the grain lines on the correct grain of the fabric. Cut out the fabric, closely following the edge of the paper pattern piece.
3 Transfer all pattern markings.

Paul Williams

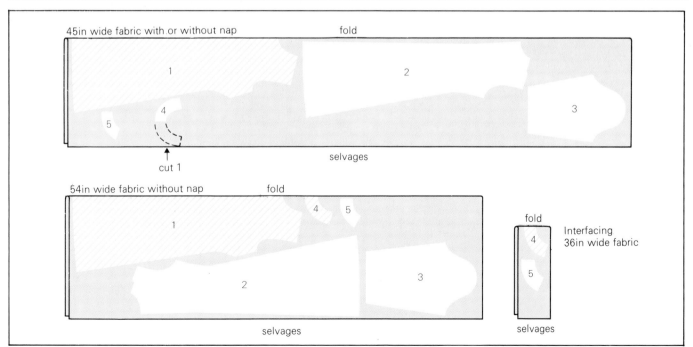

45in wide fabric with or without nap   fold

1   2

4   3

5

↑ cut 1

selvages

54in wide fabric without nap   fold

1   4   5

fold

2   3

Interfacing
36in wide fabric

4

5

selvages   selvages

Gary Warren

Brian Mayor

Fitting and interfacing

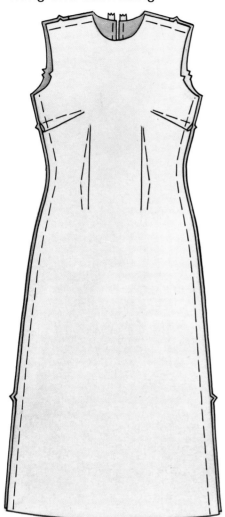

1 Pin and baste the bust and waist darts and the shoulder and side seams. Baste in the zipper.
2 Try on the dress and pin and mark any fitting adjustments on the garment.
3 Remove the basting from shoulder and side seams and darts. Press all pieces flat on the wrong side.

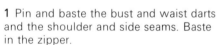

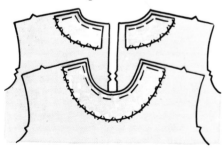

4 Trim ⅝in (1.5cm) off the center back edge of the interfacing. This will reduce the bulk at the center back seam when the seam allowance is turned in and the zipper inserted. Baste the interfacing to the wrong side of the front and back neck edges. Catch-stitch outer curved edges and center back edges to garment.

Stitching

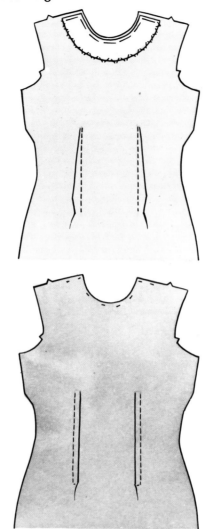

1 Fold, baste and stitch the front open-ended darts (see page 67).
On the right side, topstitch close to the outer edge of the dart seamline and across the bottom.

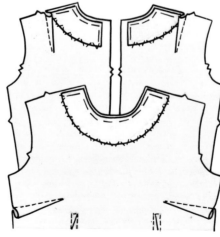

2 Fold, baste and stitch the front bust darts, and the back shoulder and waist darts. Press the bust darts down and the back darts toward the center.

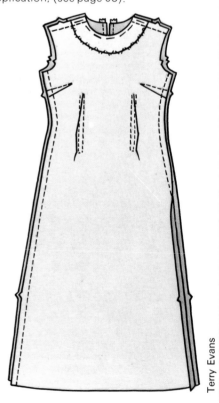

3 Baste and stitch the center back seam to circle with right sides together and notches matching. Finish and press seam open. Insert zipper into center back opening as directed for a slot application, (see page 68).

4 Baste and stitch the shoulder and side seams, with right sides together and notches matching. Trim interfacing close to stitching at the shoulder seams. Finish and press seams open.

Terry Evans

Sewing/COURSE 19

*Round neck facing
*Blind hem
*Dress: directions for
  making (2)

Round neck facing

A round neckline is one that fits smoothly around the base of the neck. The facing is cut on the same grain line as the front and back necklines of the garment, and its neck edge follows the shape of the garment neckline. It should fit the garment neckline exactly and should be inconspicuous in wear. The neck edge of a garment should be interfaced before the shoulder seams are stitched (See Sewing Course 14, Volume 3, page 68.)

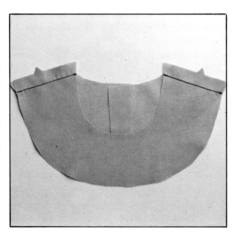

1 Baste and stitch the front and back neck facings together at the shoulder seams, with right sides together and notches matching. Press seams open.

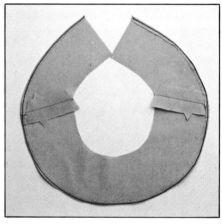

2 Finish the outer edge of the facing, but not the center back edges, using the method most suitable for the fabric. On bulky fabrics, zig-zag by machine or overcast by hand; on lightweight fabrics or those that ravel, turn under $\frac{1}{4}$in (6mm) and machine stitch. Press flat.

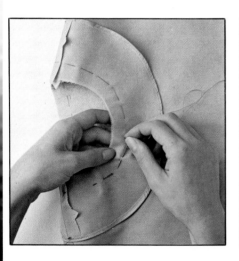

3 Pin the facing to the neckline edge of the garment, matching the raw edges, placing right sides of garment and facing together. First pin on the facing at the shoulder seams, matching the seam lines exactly. Next, match the center fronts and center backs. Pin the rest of the facing in place around the neckline. Baste the facing to the garment around the seamline at the neck edge.

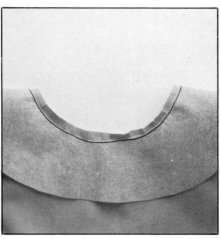

4 Stitch around the entire neck edge. Grade the seam allowance, trimming interfacing close to stitching and notch curves.

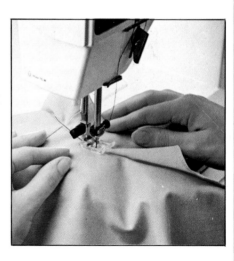

5 Press seam allowances toward facing and understitch. (If the neckline is to be topstitched, omit the understitching.)

continued

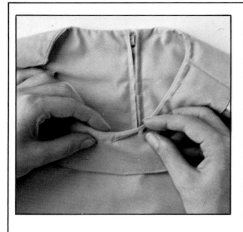

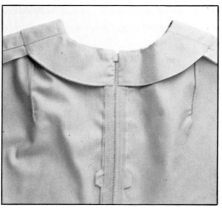

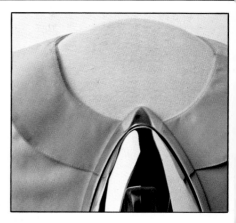

6 Turn the facing to the inside of the garment and baste close to the stitched edge, rolling the seam slightly to the wrong side.

7 On the inside, turn under the seam allowance at the center back of the facing and slip stitch the facing to the stitching over the zipper tape. Catch-stitch the facing to the shoulder seams.

8 Press the neck edge flat. If the neckline is to be topstitched, do this now, stitching $\frac{1}{4}$in (6mm) from the edge.

Blind hem

This type of hem is suitable for most fabrics ranging from cottons to heavy woolens. It has the advantage of being strong in wear and almost invisible on the right side of the garment.

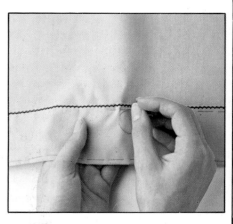

1 Turn the hem up the required amount and baste close to the folded edge. Trim hem allowance to an even width.

2 Finish the raw edge with overcasting or machine zig-zag stitching and baste the hem in place $\frac{1}{4}$in (6mm) below the finished edge.

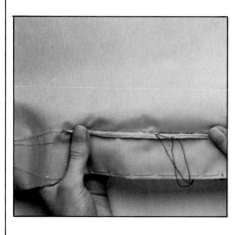

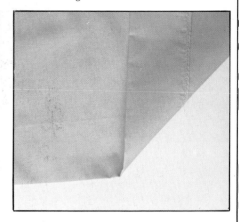

3 With the left thumb, fold back the finished edge of the hem. Working from right to left, catch-stitch the hem allowance to the garment. Do not pull the stitches too tightly.

4 Remove the basting. Press the folded edge only.

5 On the right side of the fabric, the hem stitches should not be visible.

Dress: directions for making (2)

The following directions are given for completing the dress begun on page 68.

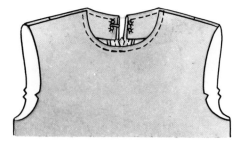

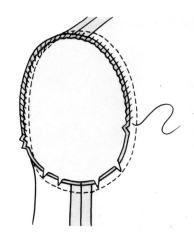

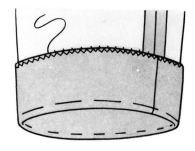

1 Apply the front and back neck facing to the dress as directed on page 71 for a round neck facing. After turning the facing to the inside and completing facing at center back, topstitch around the neck $\frac{1}{4}$in (6mm) in from edge, stitching on the right side. At the center back, sew a hook and eye to the inside edge at the top of facing.

3 Pin the sleeve into the armhole, placing right sides together. Match notches, underarm seams and the circle on the sleeve cap to the shoulder seam. Pull up ease threads to fit. Baste, spreading ease evenly. Stitch the seam, with the sleeve side up on the machine. Press seam allowances together. Clip underarm curves. Finish the seam by hand, overcasting the seam allowances together.

5 Turn up the sleeve and dress hems using the blind hem method.

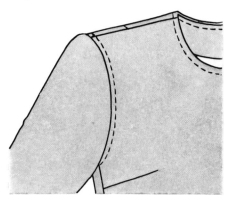

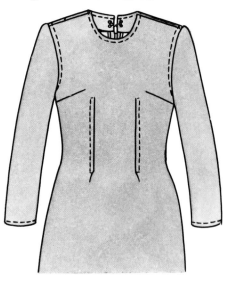

6 On the right side, topstitch $\frac{1}{4}$in (6mm) in from lower edge of sleeve.

2 Work two rows of ease stitches around the sleeve cap between notches. Baste and stitch the underarm seam of sleeve. Finish and press seam open.

4 Topstitch around armhole, stitching $\frac{1}{4}$in (6mm) in from sleeve seamline.

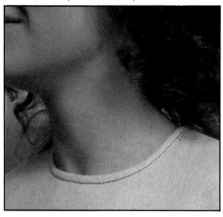

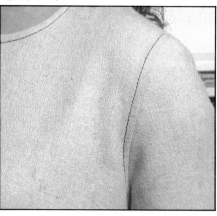

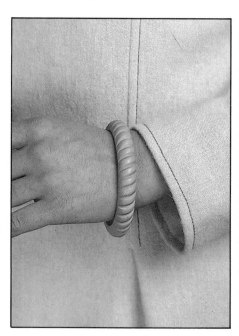

Needlework/COURSE 6

*Stem stitch
*Satin stitch
*Enlarging a design
*Transferring a design
*Blocking crewel
*Crewel tote bag

Crewel

Crewel work is a form of embroidery in which wool thread is used to make a variety of stitches on a fairly coarse fabric such as linen or cotton. The wool thread gives the work a distinctive raised appearance.

In 17th century England, crewel wool was widely used on linen for stylized flower, bird and animal designs in muted colors. Today, crewel is a far more flexible form of embroidery. Crewel wool is often combined with other threads and used in dozens of stitches to create highly original, almost three-dimensional designs.

In crewel, unlike cross-stitch, the stitches may be placed at random on the background fabric, permitting great freedom in design. And unlike needlepoint, they need cover only as much of the background fabric as the embroiderer chooses.

In this course we will introduce you to two basic stitches—all that you need to complete a handy and colorful tote bag. The course will also teach you two other useful skills: how to enlarge a design without the help of a photocopier; and how to transfer a design to fabric ready for embroidery.

Stem stitch

The stem stitch, which is sometimes called the crewel stitch, is a versatile stitch widely used in crewel work. It may be used to outline forms or to fill rectangles by placing rows of stitches close together. Circles can be filled by running a line of stitches around and around in a spiral from the center out.

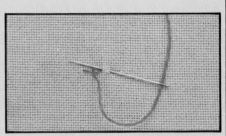

1 Work from left to right. Bring needle up at beginning of first stitch. Insert needle where stitch is to end, bringing it up halfway along the length of the first stitch and close to it to start the second stitch.

2 Insert needle at end of second stitch and bring it up again through hole where first stitch ended. Continue in a line, making as many stitches as needed.

Satin stitch

Satin stitch is another basic and very old stitch widely used in many forms of embroidery including crewel. It is a simple straight stitch used for filling small areas. To be effective, it must be done carefully so the edges of the filled area are even. The stitch may be done straight or on a slant. It is easier to keep the edges of the filled area even when the stitches are slanted.

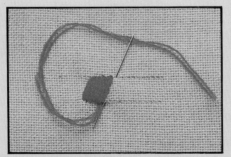

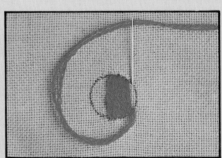

1 Bring the needle up at one edge of the area to be filled. Insert it on the opposite side at an angle if possible and bring it up again as close as possible to the beginning of the previous stitch. Insert it next to the end of the previous stitch and continue, lining up stitches as close together as possible.

2 In filling circles, start at the center and work out to one side. Return to the center and work out to the other side.

Enlarging (or reducing) a design

1 Draw a vertical line through the center of the design. Then draw additional vertical lines dividing each half evenly into quarters, each quarter into eighths, etc. Draw the same number of horizontal lines.

2 Draw a square or rectangle the size you want the design to be, keeping the proportions the same as in the original design. Draw a grid over it, using the same number of horizontal and vertical lines you drew over the original design.

3 Copy the design in each box of the grid on the original design into the corresponding box on the new grid. Trace the enlarged design. You may use the same procedure to reduce a design.

Transferring a design to fabric

1 Anchor fabric, face up, on a hard surface with masking tape.

2 Place dressmaker's carbon paper on top of the fabric with waxed side down.

3 Position design carefully and trace, using a ballpoint pen.

Frederick Mancini

Blocking

Pressing may restore crewel work to its original shape. Place it face down on a folded towel or blanket and press from the center out to the edges with a steam iron. Do not slide the iron. Press lightly, raise and move it.

If your crewel needs blocking, wet it with cold water and place it on a flat wood surface covered with several layers of a sheet. Place right side up if it has raised stitches and down if stitches are flat. Tack the corners with thumb tacks, making sure corners are square and edges parallel. Continue tacking as for needlepoint. Leave to dry.

Key	
Stitch	
A	satin stitch
B	stem stitch
C	straight stitch
Thread	
1	rust crewel wool
2	green crewel wool
3	beige crewel wool
4	gold crewel wool
5	brown crewel wool
6	rust embroidery floss
7	gold embroidery floss
8	green embroidery floss

John Hutchinson

Tote full of posies

Put traditional crewel design to modern use in this handy up-to-date tote bag.

Size: 14¼in (36cm) wide by 14¼in (36cm) deep ; strap 33in (84cm).

Materials
2yds (1.9m) of 36in (90cm)-wide
strong cotton fabric in green
Yardstick
Pencil or tailor's chalk
Scissors
Tracing paper and pencil
Dressmaker's carbon paper
Ballpoint pen or tracing wheel
Embroidery hoop (6-7in [15-17.5cm])
Crewel wool : 30yds (30m) each of
rust, green, beige, gold, and brown
Stranded cotton embroidery floss :
9yds (8m) each of rust, gold and
green
No. 7 crewel needle
Sewing thread to match background
fabric

To make
1 Trace design on page 76 and enlarge it to 9¾×9¾in (25×25cm) following directions on the same page.
2 Cut out 4 panels 13¾ × 14⅝in (35 × 37cm) and two strips 3 × 72in (7.5 ×

Simon Butcher

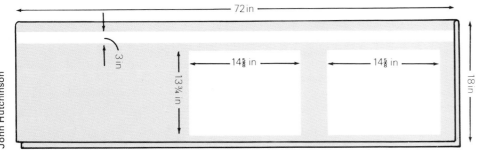

John Hutchinson

183cm) from the green material.
3 Fold one panel horizontally and then vertically to find the center and mark it with tailor's chalk.
4 Mark the center of the enlarged design.
5 Place panel on a flat surface with its longer sides running vertically. Matching the centers of the panel and the design, transfer the design to the panel following directions on page 76.
6 Center marked panel in embroidery hoop.
7 Starting at the center and working out, embroider the panel using stitches and threads indicated on the design and in key. Straight stitches are ordinary stitches as in sewing with space between them. They can be placed in a circle or a line or scattered. Secure each thread with a knot at the beginning and with a tiny

backstitch into the back of an existing stitch at the end. Do not carry thread more than about an inch (2.5cm) across the back because it will distort the fabric.
8 When the embroidery is completed, place it face down on a soft surface and press with a steam iron or a dry iron and a wet cloth. The panel should return to its original shape. If not, it should be blocked (see page 76).
9 When the embroidered panel is completely dry, lay it face up on a flat surface. Using a saucer as a pattern, round off one of the bottom corners with a pencil. Fold the panel in half lengthwise with penciled corner on top and match sides and corners. Pin together. Cut along pencil line. Round off the bottom corners of the other three panels to match the embroidered panel.

10 With right sides together, pin, baste and stitch the short ends of one long strip to form a circle. Join the short ends of the second strip in the same way. Press seams open.
11 With right sides together and with the seam on one circle matching the center of the bottom edge of the embroidered panel, baste strip to bottom and side edges of the panel leaving ⅝in (1.5cm) seam allowances. Stitch from the center of the bottom of the panel around each side stopping ⅝in (1.5cm) from the top corners on both sides. Clip corners as necessary and press seam allowance toward strip.
12 Join another panel to the other edge of the strip in the same way. This completes the outer bag.
13 Join remaining two panels to remaining strip to complete the inner bag.
14 Place inner bag inside outer bag, wrong sides together. Fold down ⅝in (1.5cm) seam allowance along upper edges to the inside between the 2 bags, pin and baste. Top stitch the 2 bags together along the upper edges by machine or slip stitch by hand.
15 Turn in seam allowances along the edges of the strap, pin and baste. Top stitch by machine or hand slip stitch together.

Crochet

Big is beautiful

This roomy and versatile coat is worked in an attractive open pattern to provide warmth without weight.

Sizes
To fit 32/34[36/38]in (83/87[92/97]cm) bust.
Length when hanging, 35in (90cm).
Sleeve seam, 18in (46cm).

Note Directions for the larger size are in brackets []; where there is only one set of figures it applies to both sizes.

Materials
46[50]oz (1280[1400]g) of a knitting worsted
Size I and wooden size 13(6.00 and 8.00mm) hooks, 5 buttons

Gauge
10 sts to 4¼in (11cm) and 10 rows to 6in (15cm) in patt on size 13 (8.00mm) hook.

Right half
**Using size 13 (8.00mm) hook chain 22 for lower edge of sleeve.
Base row 1dc into 3rd ch from hook, *1hdc into next ch, 1dc into next ch, rep from * to last ch, 1hdc into last ch. Turn. 21 sts. Beg patt.
1st row (WS) 2ch to count as first hdc, *work around next dc by working yo, insert hook from back to front between next 2 sts, around dc and through work from front to back, draw yarn through and complete dc in usual way—called double around back (dc around Bk), 1hdc into next hdc, rep from * to end, working last hdc into turning ch. Turn.
2nd row 2ch, work 1dc and 1hdc into first hdc for inc, *work around next dc by working yo, insert hook from front to back between next 2 sts, around dc and through work from back to front, draw yarn through and complete dc in usual way—called double around front (dc around Ft), 1hdc into next hdc, rep from * to last dc, 1dc around Ft, 1hdc, 1dc and 1hdc all into last hdc for inc. Turn.
Rep last 2 rows until 24 rows in all have been worked and there are 65 sts; end with first patt row. This completes sleeve.
Using separate ball of yarn chain 48 loosely and leave aside.

Next row Chain 49 loosely, 1dc into 3rd ch from hook, (1hdc into next ch, 1dc into next ch) to end of ch, then work across sleeve, 1hdc into next hdc, *1dc around Ft, 1hdc into next hdc, rep from * to end, do not turn but work across 48ch, working (1dc into next ch, 1hdc into next ch) to end. Turn. 161 sts.
Next row 2ch, *work 1dc around Bk, 1hdc into next hdc, rep from * to end.
Next row 2ch, * work, 1dc around Ft, 1hdc into next hdc, rep from * to end. Turn.
Rep these 2 rows 5[6] times more.**
Divide for neck
Next row Patt across 79 sts, turn. Patt 6 rows for right back. Fasten off. With WS facing skip next 7 sts for neck, rejoin yarn to next st, 2ch, patt to end. Turn. 75 sts. Patt 6 rows for right front.
Fasten off.

Left half
Work as for right half from ** to **.
Divide for neck
Next row Patt across first 75 sts, turn. Patt 6 rows for left front. Fasten off. With WS facing skip next 7 sts for neck, rejoin yarn to next st, 2ch, patt to end. Turn. 79 sts.
Patt 6 rows for left back.
Do not fasten off. Join backs placing WS tog, into first st on last row of right back, 1ch, work row of crab st (sc worked from left to right) through double thickness to top of neck.
Fasten off.

To finish
Join side and sleeve seams with crab st in the same way as back.

Collar
With WS facing join yarn to top of left front neck and using size 13 (8.00mm) hook work 1sc into each end around neck, working 3sc tog at each corner. Turn. 39sc.
Next row 2ch, *1dc into next sc, 1hdc into next sc, rep from * to end. Turn. Work 2 rows patt as on back and fronts. Change to size I (6.00mm) hook.
Edging
Work row of sc evenly along left front to lower edge, turn, 2 rows sc, so ending at lower edge, do not turn, change to size 13 (8.00mm) hook, 1sc into each st along lower edge, do not turn, change to size I (6.00mm) hook and work row of sc evenly along right front edge to top of collar, turn.

Serge Krouglikoff

Buttonhole row 2ch, 1sc into each of next 23sc, 3ch, skip next 2sc, (1sc into each of next 9sc, 3ch, skip next 2sc) 4 times, 1sc into each sc to end. Turn.
Next row Work 1sc into each sc and 2sc into each buttonhole to end. Do not turn but work row of crab st all around outer edge working into each sc. Fasten off.

Cuffs (alike)
Join on yarn and using size I (6.00mm) hook work 1sc into each ch around lower edge of sleeve. Do not turn but work row of crab st. Fasten off.
Sew on buttons.

Technique tip
Multiple increasing

When working several sections of a garment all in one piece you will often need to work a multiple increase when you begin a new section. In the coat you start at the cuff edge and work to the center back and the front edge, working a multiple increase when you begin the main sections.

To work a multiple increase at the beginning of the row, work a length of chain for the number of stitches you wish to add, plus extra chains for the first stitch. (The number of chains depends on the stitch being used.)

Pattern into the chain made, then pattern across the main section.

To work a multiple increase at the end of the row join on a separate ball of yarn and work a length of chain for the number of stitches you wish to add. (You will not need any extra chains for the first stitch in this case.) Fasten off the yarn.

Pattern across the main section, then pattern into each chain you have made.

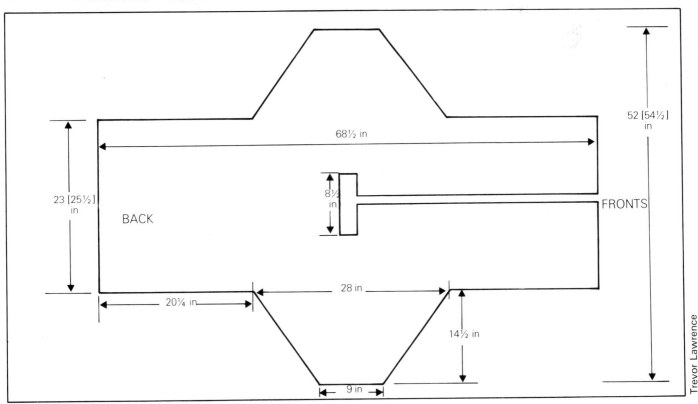

BACK

FRONTS

68½ in

52 [54½] in

23 [25½] in

8½ in

20¼ in

28 in

14½ in

9 in

EXTRA SPECIAL Crochet

Crochet casual

A rib-style stitch accentuates the vertical lines of this comfortable cardigan for a man. Two rows of single crochet finish the edges.

Sizes
To fit 38[40:42:44]in (97[102:107:112] cm) chest.
Length, 23½[23½:24¼:24¼]in (60[60:62: 62]cm).
Sleeve seam, 18¾in (48cm).

Note Directions for larger sizes are in brackets []; where there is only one set of figures it applies to all sizes.

Materials
36[37:38:39]oz (1000[1025:1075: 1100]g) of a sport yarn
Size F (4.00mm) crochet hook
5 buttons

Gauge
2 patt reps (12 sts) to 2¾in (7cm).

Back
Using size F (4.00mm) hook make 87[93:99:105] ch.
Base row Work 1dc into the 4th ch, from the hook, 1dc into each ch to end. Turn. 85[91:97:103] sts.
Next row 2ch, to count as first hdc, 1hdc into next dc, *work around each of next 3dc by working yo, insert hook from front to back, between next 2dc, around dc at left and through work from back to front, draw yarn through and complete dc in usual way—called 1 double around front (dc around Ft), 1hdc into each of next 3dc, rep from * to end, but finish last rep with 2hdc. Turn. Beg patt.
1st patt row (WS) 2ch to count as first hdc, work 1hdc into each st to end. Turn.
2nd patt row 2ch to count as first hdc, 1hdc into next dc, *work 3dc around Ft, now work 1hdc into each of next 3 sts, rep from * to end, but finish last rep with 2hdc. Turn.
These 2 rows form patt. Cont in patt until work measures 14½[14½:15:15]in (37[37:38:38]cm) from beg.
Shape armhole
Dec one st at each end of next 6 rows. 73[79:85:91] sts.
Cont without shaping until work measures 22¾[22¾:23½:23½]in (58[58:60:60]cm) from beg; end with 2nd patt row.
Shape shoulders
1st row Sl st over first 7 sts, 2ch, 1sc into each of next 5 sts, 1hdc into each st until 12 sts rem unworked, 1sc into each of next 6 sts. Fasten off.
2nd row Skip first 10 sts, rejoin yarn to next st, 2ch, 1sc into each of next 3 sts, patt until 13 sts rem, 1sc into each of next

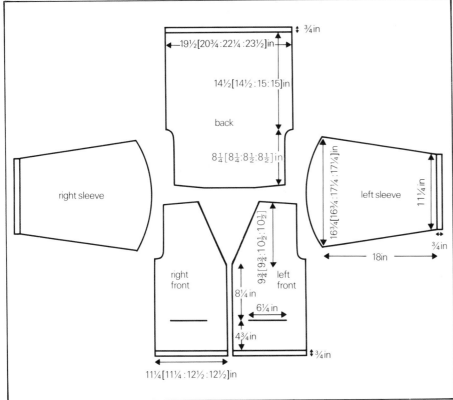

Victor Yuan

Brian Mayor

3 sts. Fasten off.

Pocket linings (make 2)
Using size F (4.00mm) hook chain 27.
Base row 1hdc into 3rd ch from hook, 1hdc into each ch to end. Turn. 26 sts. Cont in patt until work measures 4¼in (11cm). Fasten off.

Right front
Using size F (4.00mm) hook chain 51[51:57:57].
Base row Work 1dc into 4th ch from hook, 1dc into each ch to end. Turn. 49[49:55:55] sts.
Next row 2ch to count as first hdc, 1hdc into next dc, *work 3dc around Ft, 1hdc into each of next 3dc, rep from * to end. Turn. Cont in patt as for back until work measures 4¾in (12cm) from beg; end with 2nd patt row.
Pocket row 2ch to count as first hdc, work 1hdc into each of next 6[6:12:12] sts, skip next 26 sts of front and work across 26 sts of one pocket lining, patt to end. Turn. Cont in patt until work measures 13in (33cm) from beg.
Shape front edge
Dec one st at front edge on next and every other row until 46[46:51:51] sts rem.
Shape armhole
Cont to dec one st at front edge on every other row and *at same time* dec one st at armhole edge on next 6 rows. 37[37:42:42] sts. Keeping armhole edge straight cont to dec at front edge on every other row until 25[25:26:26] sts rem. Cont straight until work measures 22¾[22¾:23½:23½]in (58[58:60:60]cm) from beg; end with 2nd patt row.
Shape shoulder
1st row 2ch to count as first hdc, 1hdc into each of next 13[13:14:14] sts, 1sc into each of next 6 sts. Fasten off.
2nd row Skip first 10 sts, rejoin yarn to next st, 2ch, 1dc into each of next 3 sts, patt to end. Fasten off.
Mark 5 button positions on this front, the first 1¼in (3cm) from lower edge, the last ½in (1cm) below beg of front shaping and others equally spaced between.

Left front
Using size F (4.00mm) hook chain 51[51:57:57]. Work as for right front until first button position has been reached; end with 2nd patt row.
1st buttonhole row 2ch to count as first hdc, 1hdc into next hdc, 2ch, skip next 2 sts, 1hdc into each st to end. Turn.
2nd buttonhole row Patt to last 5 sts, 1dc around Ft, 1hdc into each of 2ch, 1hdc into each of last 2hdc. Complete to match right front, reversing all shaping and making buttonholes to correspond with markers.

Sleeves
Using size F (4.00mm) hook chain 51.
Base row Work 1dc into 4th ch from hook,

1dc into each ch to end. Turn. 49 sts.
Next row 2ch to count as first hdc, 1hdc into each of next 2dc, *work 3dc around Ft, 1hdc into each of next 3dc, rep from * to end, but finish last rep with 2hdc. Turn. Cont in patt as for back but inc one st at each end of 3rd row, then at each end of every foll 4th row until there are 73[73:75:75] sts. Cont straight until work measures 18in (46cm) from beg; end with 2nd patt row.
Shape top
Dec one st at each end of next 6 rows. Fasten off.

To finish
Press with warm iron over damp cloth. Join shoulder seams. Set in sleeves, then join side and sleeve seams. Work 4 rows of sc evenly around lower edge of each sleeve and along top edge of each pocket. Work one row of sc evenly all around outer edge. Turn. Work 3 more rows in sc working 3sc into each corner sc. Sew down pocket linings and ends of pocket tops.
Press seams and edgings.
Sew on buttons to correspond with buttonholes.

Technique tip
Working a buttonhole in the main fabric

Sometimes you may need to work buttonholes in the main fabric as you are working the front. If there are two or more buttonholes to be worked, you should first work the section carrying the buttons—in the case of a man's garment, the right front. The button positions are then marked on this front section and the buttonholes are worked on the second front to correspond with the markers. In this cardigan the buttonholes are worked in the pattern, rather than in the border, and should be worked as follows.

End the last row before the buttonhole row at the front edge. To work the buttonhole, pattern across the first 2 half doubles, work 2 chains for the top of the buttonhole.

Skip the next 2 stitches for the base of the buttonhole, pattern to the end of the row.

On the second row you need to work into the chains at the top of the buttonholes. Pattern to within the last 5 stitches: that is, to within the first half double before the 2 chains, the 2 chains and the last 2 half doubles.

Pattern around next half double, work 1 half double into each of the 2 chains, then work 1 half double into each of the last 2 half doubles. This completes the first buttonhole. Continue to work the pattern on the front of the garment until you reach the position of the next button. Work the next buttonhole as described here to correspond with the position of that button, keeping the pattern across the garment as before.

Coral Mula

Serge Krouglikoff

EXTRA SPECIAL CROCHET

Well suited

This smart vest and skirt, with their softly textured bands of patterns, can be worn together or separately, as you like.

Sizes
Vest to fit 32[34:36:38]in (83[87:92:97]cm) bust. Length, 19[19½:20½:21]in (49[50:52:53]cm).
Skirt to suit 34[36:38:40]in (87[92:97:102]cm) hips. Length, 30in (76cm).

Note Directions for the larger sizes are in brackets []; where there is only one set of figures it applies to all sizes.

Materials
20[22:23:25]oz (550[600:650:700]g) of a sport yarn
Size E (3.50mm) crochet hook

Gauge
18 sts and 15 rows to 4in (10cm) in main patt on size E (3.50mm) hook.

Vest

Back
Make 85[89:93:97] ch.
Base row 1sc into 2nd ch from hook, 1sc into each ch. Turn. 84[88:92:96]sc.
Next row 2ch to count as first hdc, skip first sc, *2hdc into next sc, skip next sc, rep from * to last sc, 1hdc into last sc. Turn. Beg patt.
1st row 2ch, 1hdc into sp between last hdc of last row and next grp, *2hdc into sp

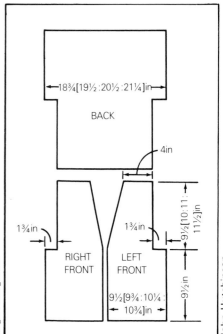

18¾[19½:20½:21¼]in

BACK

4in

RIGHT FRONT

LEFT FRONT

1¾in

1¾in

1¾in

9½[10:11:11½]in

9½in

9½in

9½[9¾:10¼:10¾]in

John Hutchinson

between next 2 grp, rep from * ending with 2hdc between last grp and 2ch. Turn. 42[44:46:48] 2-hdc grp.

2nd row 2ch, skip first 2hdc, *hdc into sp between next 2 grp, rep from * to last grp, 1hdc into top of 2ch. Turn. 41[43:45:47] grp with hdc at each end. These 2 rows form main patt. Work 34 more rows; end with 2nd row.

Shape armholes

Next row Sl st across first sp, next 4 grp and into next sp, 2ch, 1hdc into same sp, patt as first row to last 4 grp, turn. 68[72:76:80] sts. Cont in patt without shaping until work measures 19[19½:20½:21]in (49[50:52:53]cm) from beg. Fasten off.

Left front

Using size E (3.50mm) hook make 43[45:47:49] ch. Work base row as for back. 42[44:46:48] sc. Cont as for back until work measures same as back to armholes.

Shape armhole

Next row Sl st across first sp, next 4 grp and into next sp, 2ch, 1hdc into same sp, patt to end. Turn. 34[36:38:40] sts.

Shape front edge

1st row 2ch, 1hdc into next sp, *2hdc into next sp, rep from * ending with 1hdc into top of 2ch. Turn. 33[35:37:39] sts.

2nd row Work as for first patt row to last 2 sts, 1hdc into 2nd of 2ch. Turn. 33[35:37:39] sts.

3rd row 2ch, skip first sp, *2hdc into next sp, rep from * ending with 1hdc into top of 2ch. Turn. 32[34:36:38] sts.

4th row Work as for first patt row, ending with 2hdc into last sp. Turn. 32[34:36:38] sts.

Rep last 4 rows, dec one st on every alternate row until 20 sts rem. Cont without shaping until front measures same as back to shoulders. Fasten off.

Right front

Work as given for left front to armhole.

Shape armhole

Next row Patt to last 4 grp, turn.

Shape front edge

1st row Work as for 2nd patt row to last sp, 1hdc into sp; leaving last loop of each on hook, work 1hdc into same place and 1hdc into top of 2ch, yo and draw through all loops on hook. Turn.

2nd row 2ch, skip first 2 sts, *2hdc into next sp, rep from * ending as first patt row. Turn.

3rd row As 2nd patt row, ending with 1hdc only into last sp. Turn.

4th row Work as for first patt row. Rep last 4 rows, dec one st on every alternate row until 20 sts rem. Complete to match left front.

To finish

Join side and shoulder seams.

Front border

With RS of work facing and using size E

(3.50mm) hook, join yarn to first row end at lower edge of right front, 1sc into same row end, 1sc into each row end to beg of neck shaping, 3sc into next row end, 1sc into each row end of neck shaping, 1sc into each grp and into each sp along back neck, cont down left front edge in same way. Turn.

Next row 3ch to count as first dc, skip first st, *leaving last loop of each on hook work 3dc into next st, yo and draw through all loops on hook—called cluster, 1ch, skip next st, rep from * all around, ending at lower edge of left front with 1dc into last st. Turn.

Next row 1ch to count as first sc, 1sc into first dc, *1sc into sp, 1sc into cluster, rep from * all around, ending with 1sc into last dc, do not turn, work 2 more sc into same dc then cont along lower edge working 1sc into each foundation ch. Join with sl st to first sc on right front edge. Fasten off.

Armhole edgings (alike)

Work one row of single crochet evenly around armhole.

Skirt

Using size E (3.50mm) hook make 170[180:188:198] ch for entire top edge.

Base row 1dc into 4th ch from hook, 1dc into each ch to end. Turn. 168[178:186:196] sts.

Next row 3ch to count as first dc, skip first dc, 1dc into each dc, ending with 1dc into top of 3ch. Turn.

Rep last row 8 times more.

11th row 3ch, skip first st, *skip 1st, working into back loop only of each st,

work 3dc into next st leaving last loop of each on hook, yo and draw through all loops on hook—called cluster, 1ch, rep from * to last st, 1dc into last st. Turn.

12th row 1ch, *1sc into sp, 1sc into cluster, rep from * ending with 1sc into top of 3ch. Turn.

13th row 3ch, skip 1sc, *skip 1sc, working into both loops of each st as normal, work cluster into next st, 1ch, rep from * to last st, 1dc into last st. Turn.

14th row As 12th. 168[178:186:196] sts.

15th row 2ch to count as first hdc, skip first sc, *2hdc into next sc, skip 1sc, rep from * to last sc, 1hdc into last sc. Turn.

16th row 2ch, 1hdc into sp between last hdc of last row and next grp, *2hdc into sp between next 2grp, rep from * ending with 2hdc between last grp and 2ch. Turn.

17th row 2ch, skip first 2hdc, *2hdc into sp between next 2grp, rep from * to last grp, 1hdc into top of 2ch. Turn.

Rep 16th and 17th rows 4 times more, then 16th row again. Rep 11th to 14th rows. Rep last 30 rows twice more, then work 6 rows in dc. Fasten off.

To finish

Join back seam. Press with a warm iron over a damp cloth. Turn first 4 rows of foundation edge to WS to form casing at waist and sl st in position.

Tie Using size E (3.50mm) hook chain 9.

Base row 1sc into 2nd ch from hook, 1sc into each ch to end. Turn.

Next row 1ch, 1sc into each sc. Turn.

Rep last row until tie measures 59in (150cm) or required length. Fasten off. Thread tie through waist casing through center at front. Tie in a bow.

Technique tip

Lining the skirt

To help the hang of the skirt it is advisable either to wear a slip or line the skirt.

If you wish to line the skirt you will need 1[1¼:1½:1½]yd (1[1.1:1.2:1.2]m) of 36in (90cm)-wide lining fabric, matching thread and a needle.

Cut fabric into a rectangle measuring 38[40:42:44]in (96[100:106:110]cm) by 31in (79cm); this allows ⅝in (1.5cm) on each side for center back seam, ¾in (2cm) for upper hem and 2¾in (7cm) for lower hem.

Sew center back seam, press open and finish seam allowances by turning under edges and hemming. Turn up 1¼in (3cm) hem, then 1½in (4cm) at lower edge.

Press under ¾in (2cm) hem along upper edge. Finish raw edge then slip stitch folded edge to lower edge of waistband on skirt before inserting ties into casing.

Terry Evans

Shoestring

Sewing box

Transform an old cigar box into a pretty sewing box with a place for pins, thread and odds and ends.

Di Lewis

Materials

Cigar box about 8½ × 5½ in (22 × 14cm) and 2¾in (7cm) deep
⅝yd (.5m) of 36in (90cm)-wide print fabric
⅜yd (.3m) of 36in (90cm)-wide plain fabric for lining
Scraps of thick cardboard
⅝yd (.5m) of 36in (90cm)-wide lightweight batting
Strong glue
¼yd (.2m) of ⅜in (1cm)-wide elastic
Matching thread
Round button ¾in (2cm) in diameter

1 Cut out and glue pieces of batting to the top and to the four outside edges of the cigar box.

2 Measure around the outside of the box widthwise and lengthwise. Add 1½in (4cm) to these two measurements and cut a rectangle this size from print fabric for outside covering.

3 Place the box on the wrong side of this fabric piece. Apply glue to the inside edges of the lid and to the front and side inside edges of the box. Glue the fabric in place on the box, mitering the fabric at the corners of the lid and at the sides of the box itself. Trim away excess fabric. Sew the fabric together at the miters.

4 Cut a strip of print fabric 2¼in (6cm) wide by the width of the back of the box. Glue this strip in place on the inside of the box over the hinges, turning under the raw edges to finish them. Leave the box to dry.

5 Measure the inside of the sides and the inside base of the box, allowing for the lid closing. Draw these pieces on thick cardboard and cut out.

6 Cut out and glue a piece of batting the same size as the cardboard pieces to one side of each piece. Place these pieces in the box and trim away excess cardboard until the pieces fit correctly.

7 Cut out a piece of plain lining fabric ¾in (2cm) larger all around than each padded cardboard piece. On each piece, place the fabric over the batting and gather the raw edges of the fabric. using long stitches on the underside.

8 Cut a piece of plain lining fabric 1¼in (3cm) wide by the length of the back of the box plus 4in (10cm). Fold this strip in half lengthwise with right sides together. Pin, baste and stitch along the strip ¼in (5mm) from raw edges. Turn strip right side out. Thread elastic through strip, pinning the ends of elastic and fabric together. Position the elastic strip on the right side of the back of the covered lining piece. Fold the raw ends of the elastic strip under on the wrong side and sew them in place.

9 Stitch the four side pieces together down the short sides with right sides facing in.

10 Glue the covered base in position in the box. Glue the covered sides in position in the box.

11 Cut a rectangle of plain lining fabric the same size as the box lid. Cut a rectangle of batting the same size as the fabric. Pin and baste the batting to the wrong side of the fabric. Turn under ⅜in (1cm) on all edges; pin and baste. Topstitch across the fabric both ways to form 1¼in (3cm) squares. Glue the padded fabric in place, centering it on the inside of the lid. When the glue has dried, slip stitch in place.

12 Sew the button to the right side of the lid in the center of the front edge.

Geometrical class

Put clean lines, bold blocks of color and soft mohair together, and the result is a sweater that will earn you straight A's for your fashion sense.

Sizes
To fit 32[34:36:38]in (82[87:92:97]cm) bust.
Length, 26in (66cm).
Sleeve seam, 22in (56cm).
Note Directions for larger sizes are in brackets []; where there is only one set of figures it applies to all sizes.

Materials
6[7:7:7]oz (160[200:200:200]g) of a medium-weight mohair in main color (A)
5[5:6:6]oz (120[120:160:160]g) in first contrasting color (B)
5[5:5:6]oz (120[120:120:160]g) in 2nd contrasting color (C)
6oz (160g) in 3rd contrasting color (D)
1 pair each Nos. 6, 8 and 10 (4½, 5½ and 6½mm) needles

Gauge
16 sts to 4in (10cm) in stockinette st using No. 8 (5½mm) needles.

Back
**Using No. 6 (4½mm) needles and A, cast on 66[70:74:78] sts.
1st ribbing row K2, *P2, K2, rep from * to end of row.
2nd ribbing row P2, *K2, P2, rep from * to end.
Rep these 2 rows for 4in (10cm): end with first ribbing row.
Next row Rib 7[9:10:12], (pick up loop lying between sts and work into back of it—called M1—rib 17[17:18:18] sts) 3 times, M1, rib 8[10:10:12] sts. 70[74:78:82] sts.
Change to No. 8 (5½mm) needles.
Twisting yarn when changing color to

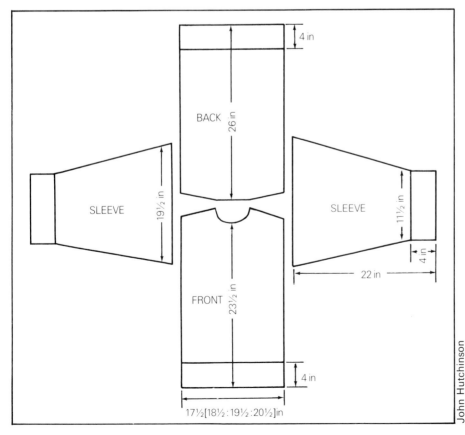

John Hutchinson

avoid a hole, cont in stockinette st as foll:
1st row K21[23:25:27] sts in B, 3 in A
and 46[48:50:52] in C.
2nd row P46[48:50:52] sts in C, 3 in A
and 21[23:25:27] in B.
Rep these 2 rows until work measures
11½in (29cm) from beg; end with WS
row. Cut off all colors.
Join on A; beg with a K row, work 4 rows
stockinette st.
Next row K46[48:50:52] in D, 3 in A and
21[23:25:27] in B.
Next row P21[23:25:27] in B, 3 in A
and 46[48:50:52] in D.
Rep the last 2 rows until work measures
17¼in (44cm) from beg; end with WS
row. Cut off all colors.
Join on A: beg with a K row, work 4 rows
stockinette st.
Next row K21[23:25:27] in C, 3 in A
and 46[48:50:52] in D.
Next row P46[48:50:52] in D, 3 in A
and 21[23:25:27] in C.**
Rep the last 2 rows until work measures
26in (66cm) from beg; end with WS row.
Shape shoulders
Cont in colors as set, bind off 6[7:8:9] sts
at beg of next 2 rows and 6 sts at beg of
foll 6 rows.
Cut off yarn and leave rem 22[24:26:28]
sts on a holder.

Front
Work as for back from ** to **
Rep last 2 rows until work measures
23½in (60cm) from beg; end with WS
row.
Divide for neck
Cont in colors as set, work thus:
Next row Work 27[28:29:30], K2 tog,
turn and complete this side first.
Dec one st at neck edge on every row
until 24[25:26:27] sts rem. Cont without
shaping until work measures same as
back to shoulder shaping, ending at
armhole edge.
Shape shoulder
Bind off 6[7:8:9] sts at beg of next row
and 6 sts at beg of foll 3 alternate rows.
Return to rem sts and place center
12[14:16:18] sts on a holder. Rejoin D
to rem sts at neck edge, K2 tog, work to
end of row.
Complete to match first side reversing
shaping.

Left sleeve
Using No. 6 (4½mm) needles and A, cast
on 46 sts. Work 2 ribbing rows of back for
4in (10cm); end with first ribbing row.
Next row Rib 4, (M1, rib 1) 36 times, rib
2. 78 sts.
Change to No. 8 (5½mm) needles.
Twisting yarn when changing color to
avoid a hole, cont in stockinette st as foll:
1st row K25 in B, 3 in A and 50 in C.
2nd row P50 in C, 3 in A and 25 in B.
Rep these 2 rows until work measures
9in (23cm) from beg; end with WS row.
Cut off all colors.

Gary Warren

Join on A, beg with a K row, work 4 rows stockinette st.

Next row K50 in D, 3 in A and 25 in B.

Next row P25 in B, 3 in A and 50 in D.

Rep these 2 rows until work measures 16¼in (41cm) from beg; end with WS row. Cut off all colors.

Join on A; beg with a K row, work 4 rows stockinette st.

Next row K25 in C, 3 in A and 50 in D.

Next row P50 in D, 3 in A and 25 in C.

Rep these 2 rows until work measures 22in (56cm) from beg; end with WS row. Bind off loosely.

Right sleeve

Using No. 6 (4½mm) needles and A, cast on 46 sts. Work 2 ribbing rows of back for 4in (10cm); end with first ribbing row.

Next row Rib 4, (M1, rib 1) 36 times, rib 2. 78 sts.

Change to No. 8 (5½mm) needles. Twisting yarn when changing color to avoid a hole, cont in stockinette st as foll:

1st row K50 in B, 3 in A and 25 in C.

2nd row P25 in C, 3 in A and 50 in B.

Rep these 2 rows until work measures 9in (23cm) from beg; end with WS row. Cut off all colors.

Join on A; beg with a K row, work 4 rows stockinette st.

Next row K25 in D, 3 in A and 50 in B.

Next row P50 in B, 3 in A and 25 in D.

Rep these 2 rows until work measures 16¼in (41cm) from beg; end with WS row. Cut off all colors.

Join on A; beg with a K row, work 4 rows stockinette st.

Next row K50 in C, 3 in A and 25 in D.

Next row P25 in D, 3 in A and 50 in C.

Rep these 2 rows until work measures 22in (56cm) from beg; end with WS row. Bind off loosely.

Collar

Join right shoulder seam. With WS of work facing, using No. 6 (4½mm) needles and A, pick up and K 21 sts down left side of neck, K sts from holder, pick up and K 21 sts up right side of neck, then K back neck sts from holder. 76[80:84:88] sts.

Next row K7[9:10:2] sts, (M1, K3[3:3:4] sts) 21 times, M1, K6[8:11:2]. 98[102:106:110] sts.

Beg with ribbing row 2, rib as for back until collar measures 2¼in (6cm).

Change to No. 8 (5½mm) needles and cont in ribbing until collar measures 5¼in (13cm).

Change to No. 10 (6½mm) needles and cont in ribbing until collar measures 7½in (19cm). Bind off very loosely in ribbing.

To finish

Do not block. Join left shoulder and collar seam. Mark center of bound-off edge of sleeves with a pin, match pin to shoulder seam, then sew sleeves to back and front. Join side and sleeve seams.

Technique tip

Using separate bails of yarn in a row

When you knit blocks of color across a row you will need to twist the yarns around each other when you change color; otherwise, you will make a hole in the knitting. In the sweater we have used three colors in each row, and these should be changed as described below.

To change color on a knit row; after you have knitted the required number of stitches using the first color, hold this color to the left at the back of the work; then pick up the second color and bring it across to the right at the back of the work, under and over the top of the first color.

Knit the required number of stitches using the second color. Hold this color to the left, pick up the third color and bring it across to the right at the back of the work, under and over the top of the second color; knit to the end of the row.

To change color on a purl row: after purling the required number of stitches using the third color, hold this color across to the left at the front of the work; then pick up second color and bring it across to the right at the front of the work, under and over the top of the third color.

Purl the required number of stitches using the second color. Hold the second color across to the left at the front of the work. Pick up the first color and bring it across to the right at the front of the work, under and over the top of the second color; purl to the end of the row.

Cabled twosome

The tunic and sleeveless sweater are both worked with a crisp, two-color cable.

Sizes

Sleeveless sweater To fit 22[24:26:28]in (56[61:66:71]cm) chest.
Length, 13[14½:16:17½]in·(33[37:41: 44]cm).
Tunic To fit chest sizes as above. Length, 17[19:20½:22]in (44[48:52: 56]cm).

Note Directions for larger sizes are in brackets []; if there is only one set of figures this applies to all sizes.

Materials

Sleeveless sweater 2[4:4:4]oz (50[100:100:100]g) of a sport yarn in a dark color (A)
2oz (50g) in a light color (B)
Tunic 4[4:4:6]oz (100[100:100:150]g) of a sport yarn in a dark color (A)
2[4:4:4]oz (50[100:100:100]g) in a light color (B)
1 pair each Nos. 4 and 7 (3¾ and 5mm) knitting needles
1 cable needle (cn)

Gauge

21 sts and 26 rows to 4in (10cm) in stockinette st on No. 7 (5mm) needles.

Sleeveless sweater

Back

**Using No. 4 (3¾mm) needles and A, cast on 56[60:66:70] sts and work in K1, P1 ribbing for 2in (5cm).
Next row Rib 9[5:5:7], pick up loop between needles and work into back, called make one or M1, (rib 13[10:11:8], M1) to last 8[5:6:7] sts, rib to end. 60[66:72:78] sts. Change to No. 7 (5mm) needles.
Next row K30[33:36:39] A, join in B, K30[33:36:39] B.
Next row With B, P24[27:30:33], K2, P4, then with A, P4, K2, P24[27:30:33]. Twisting yarns when changing color to avoid a hole, beg patt.
1st row (RS) With A, K24[27:30:33], P2, K4, then with B, K4, P2, K24[27:30:33].
2nd row With B, P24[27:30:33], K2, P4, then with A, P4, K2, P24[27:30:33].
3rd–6th rows 1st and 2nd rows twice.
7th row With A, K24[27:30:33], P2, next 4 sts in A onto cn and leave at front, with B, K4, join in 2nd ball of A, using 2nd ball of A, K4 sts from cn, join in 2nd ball of B, with 2nd ball of B, P2, K24[27:30:33].
8th row With B, P24[27:30:33], K2, with A, P4, with B, P4, with A, K2, P24[27:30:33].
9th row With A, K24[27:30:33], P2, with B, K4, with A, K4, with B, P2, K24[27:30:33].
10th–19th rows Work 8th and 9th rows 5 times.
20th row As 8th row.
21st row With A, K24[27:30:33], P2, sl next 4sts in B onto cn and leave at

front, with A, K4, with B, K4 sts from cn, with B, P2, K24[27:30:33]. Cut off extra balls of A and B.
22nd row As 2nd row.
23rd–28th row Work first and 2nd rows 3 times.
These 28 rows form the patt. Cont in patt until work measures 8[9:10:11]in (20[23:25:28]cm) at center from beg; end with WS row.

Shape armholes

Bind off 6 sts at beg of next 2 rows. Dec one st at each end of every row until 44[50:56:62] sts rem, at each end of every alternate row until 38[42:46:50] sts rem.
**Cont straight until work measures 13[14½:16:17½]in (33[37:41:44]cm) at center from beg; end with WS row.

Shape shoulders

Bind off 3[4:4:5] sts at beg of next 2 rows and 4[4:5:5] sts at beg of foll 2. Put rem 24[26:28:30] sts on holder.

Front

Work as for back from ** to ** reversing colors — working B for A and A for B throughout. Cont straight until front measures 10[11½:13:14½]in (25[29:33: 37]cm) at center from beg; end with WS row.

Divide for neck

Next row K11[12:13:14], turn and leave rem sts on spare needle. Finish this side first.
Dec one st at neck edge on next and foll 3 alternate rows. 7[8:9:10] sts. Cont straight until front is same length as back up to beg of shoulder; end with a WS row.

Shape shoulder

Bind off 3[4:4:5] sts at beg of next row. Work 1 row. Bind off. Return to sts on spare needle, sl next 16[18:20:22] sts on holder, join yarn to next st and work to end of row. Match to first side.

Neck border

Join right shoulder seam. With RS facing, using No. 4 (3¾mm) needles and A, pick up and K 25 sts along left front neck, K sts from holder, pick up and K 25 sts along right front, K back sts from holder. 90[94:98:102] sts.
Work in K1, P1 ribbing for ¾in (2cm). Bind off in ribbing.

Armhole borders (alike)

Join left shoulder and neck border seam. With RS facing, using No. 4 (3¾mm) needles and A, pick up and K 70[76:82: 88] sts around armhole. Work 6 rows in K1, P1 ribbing. Bind off in ribbing.

To finish

Join side seams. Press seams.

Tunic

Back

**Using No. 4 (3¾mm) needles and A, cast on 28[30:33:35] sts, join in B and cast on 28[30:33:35] sts.
Next row K28[30:33:35] B, 28[30:33:35] A, twisting yarn at front of work when changing color to avoid a hole. Work further 6 rows garter st, twisting yarn on WS of work.
Next row Keeping colors correct, K9[5:5:7], pick up loop between needles

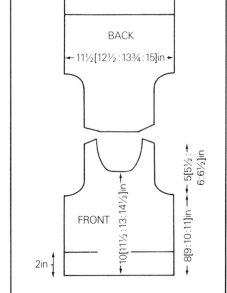

SLEEVELESS SWEATER

BACK

←11½[12½ : 13¾ : 15]in→

FRONT

2in

10[11½ : 13 : 14½]in

8[9:10:11]in

5[5½ : 6:6½]in

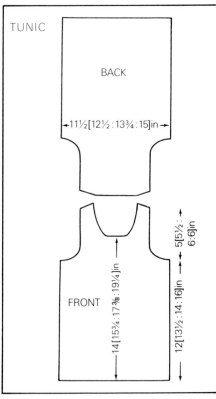

TUNIC

BACK

←11½[12½ : 13¾ : 15]in→

FRONT

14[15¾ : 17⅜ : 19¼]in

12[13½ : 14 : 16]in

5[5½ : 6:6]in

and work into back—called M1, (K13[10: 11:8], M1) to last 8[5:6:7] sts, K to end. 60[66:72:78] sts. Change to No. 7 (5mm) needles.

Next row With B, K3, P21[24:27:30], K2, P4, then with A, P4, K2, P21[24:27: 30], K3. Keeping 3 sts at each end in garter st, beg with 1st patt row, cont in patt as for sweater until back measures 4in (10cm) at center from beg. Taking garter st at each end into stockinette st, cont in patt until back measures 12[13½:14:16]in (31[34:36:40]cm) at center from beg; end with WS row.** Shape armholes as for sweater, then cont straight until back measures 17[19:20½:22]in (44[48:52: 56]cm) at center from beg; end with WS row. Shape shoulders as for sweater.

Front
Work as for back of tunic from ** to **.

Shape armholes as for sweater, cont straight until front measures 14[15¾:17¼: 19¼]in (36[40:44:49]cm) at center from beg; end with WS row.
Shape neck and shoulders as for the sweater.

Neck and armhole borders
Work as for sweater.

Belt
Using No. 4 (3¾mm) needles and A, cast on 9 sts.
1st row (RS) K2, (P1, K1) to last st, K1.
2nd row K1, (P1, K1) to end. Rep 2 rows for 34[36:38:40]in (86[91:97: 102]cm). Bind off in ribbing.

To finish
Join side seams from top of garter st borders. Press seams.

Ray Duns

A la russe

Our Russian-style coat with its matching pillbox hat will give you plenty of class. Set it off with a pencil-slim black skirt and boots, or wear it with pants for a casual, but highly sophisticated, look.

Sizes
Coat To fit 32[34:36:38]in (83[87:92:97]cm) bust.
Length, 35¼[36½:37¾:39¼]in (91[94:97:100]cm).
Sleeve seam, 17¼in (44cm).
Hat To fit average size head.

Note Directions for larger sizes are in brackets []; where there is only one set of figures it applies to all sizes.

Materials
*18[18:20:20]oz (500[500:550:550]g) of a bulky weight yarn in color A
15[16:18:18]oz (400[450:500:500]g) in color B
9[11:11:13]oz (250[300:300:350]g) in color C
11[13:13:15]oz (300[350:350:400]g) in color D
1 pair each Nos. 8 and 9 (5½ and 6mm) knitting needles
Size I (6.00mm) crochet hook
A large-eyed needle
5 toggles
3 snaps*

Gauge
13 sts and 17 rows to 4in (10cm) in stockinette st on No. 9 (6mm) needles.
14 sts and 24 rows to 4in (10cm) in garter st on No. 9 (6mm) needles.

Coat
Large squares
Using No. 9 (6mm) needles and A, cast on 25[26:27:28] sts. Beg with K row, work 35[36:37:39] rows stockinette st. Bind off dec 2 sts evenly along row. Make 3 more squares in A, then 3 in B.

Medium squares
Using No. 9 (6mm) needles and A, cast on 23[24:25:26] sts. Beg with K row, work 32[33:35:36] rows stockinette st. Bind off dec 2 sts evenly along row. Make 4 more squares in A, then 4 in B.

Small squares
Using No. 9 (6mm) needles and A, cast on 21[22:23:24] sts. Beg with K row, work 28[30:31:32] rows stockinette st. Bind off dec 2 sts evenly along row. Make 2 more squares in A, then 2 in B and 2 in C.

Blanket stitch edging
Leaving 2 medium squares in A unworked for pocket linings and using D, work blanket stitch around outer edge of each rem square.

Back bodice
Using No. 9 (6mm) needles and B, cast on 57[60:63:66] sts. Cont in garter st working in stripes of 2 rows B, 2 rows C and 2 rows A until 22 rows have been worked. Mark each end of last row to

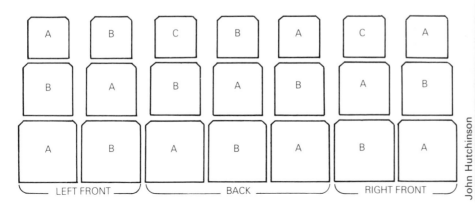

LEFT FRONT   BACK   RIGHT FRONT

John Hutchinson

denote top of side seam. Cont in stripe sequence, work a further 44[46:48:50] rows.

Shape shoulders
Bind off 4 sts at beg of next 8 rows and 4[5:6:7] sts at beg of foll 2 rows. Bind off rem 17[18:19:20] sts.

Left front bodice
Using No. 9 (6mm) needles and B, cast on 38[40:42:44] sts. Cont in garter st working in stripes as for back bodice until 22 rows have been worked. Mark end of last row to denote top of side seam. Cont in stripe sequence, work a further 33[35:37:39] rows; end at front edge.

Shape neck
Next row K7 and leave these 7 sts on a holder, bind off 5[6:7:8], K to end. 26[27:28:29] sts.
Dec one st at neck edge on next 6 rows 20[21:22:23] sts. Work 4 rows straight, so ending at side edge.

Shape shoulder
Bind off 4 sts at beg of next and foll 3 alternate rows. Work 1 row, then bind off rem 4[5:6:7] sts.
Place the 7 sts from holder onto No. 9 (6mm) needle with point at inner end, rejoin yarn and work 5 rows garter st, dec one st at neck edge on every row. K2 tog and fasten off.

Right front bodice
Using No. 9 (6mm) needles and B, cast on 38[40:42:44] sts. Cont in garter st, working in stripes as for back bodice until 22 rows have been worked. Mark beg of last row to denote top of side seam. Cont in stripe sequence, work a further 33[35:37:39] rows; end at side edge.

Shape neck
Next row K26[27:28:29], bind off 5, K to end.
Working on group of 7 sts only, work 5 rows dec one st at neck edge on every row. K2 tog and fasten off. Rejoin yarn to rem sts, dec one st at neck edge on next 6 rows 20[21:22:23] sts. Work 5 rows straight, so ending at side edge.

Shape shoulder
Bind off 4 sts at beg of next and foll 3 alternate rows. Work 1 row, then bind off rem 4[5:6:7] sts.

Sleeves
Using No. 8 (5½mm) needles and D, cast on 36[38:40:42] sts. K 8 rows.
Change to No. 9 (6mm) needles and cont in garter st inc one st at each end of 11th and 4 foll 20th rows and working in stripes of 8 rows B, 8 rows C, 8 rows A, (6 rows B, 6 rows C and 6 rows A) twice, (4 rows B, 4 rows C and 4 rows A) twice, (2 rows B, 2 rows C and 2 rows A) twice.

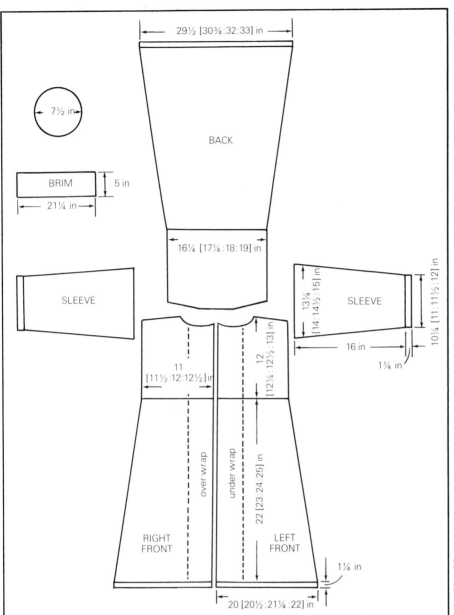

29½ [30¾ : 32 : 33] in

BACK

7½ in

BRIM   5 in

21¼ in

16¼ [17¼ : 18 : 19] in

SLEEVE

13¾ [14 : 14½ : 15] in

10¼ [11 : 11½ : 12] in

SLEEVE

16 in

1¼ in

11 [11½ : 12 : 12½] in

12 [12¼ : 12½ : 13] in

over wrap

under wrap

22 [23 : 24 : 25] in

RIGHT FRONT

LEFT FRONT

1¼ in

20 [20½ : 21¼ : 22] in

John Hutchinson

Kim Sayer

Bind off loosely.

To finish
Form back and fronts by sewing squares tog, placing them as shown in diagram. Join pocket linings to back of medium square in A on each front, leaving side edge open. Using a flat seam sew bodice to back and fronts.

Lower borders
With RS of back facing, using No. 9 (6mm) needles and D, pick up and K 75[78:81:84] sts along lower edge, working behind blanket stitch.
K5 rows. Bind off.
With RS of left front facing, using No. 9 (6mm) needles and D, pick up and K 50[52:54:56] sts along lower edge, working behind blanket stitch.
K 5 rows. Bind off.
Work right front border as for left front border.

Front edgings (alike)
Using No. 9 (6mm) needles and with RS facing join on yarn and pick up and K 103[107:111:115] sts evenly along front edge. K 1 row. Bind off.

Collar
Join shoulder seams. Using No. 9 (6mm) needles and with RS facing join on D and pick up and K 27[28:29:30] sts from right front neck, 15[16:17:18] sts from back neck and 27[28:29:30] sts from left front neck. 69[72:75:78] sts. K 9 rows. Change to No. 8 (5½mm) needles and K 8 more rows. Bind off. Sew bound-off edges of sleeves to armholes between markers, then join side and sleeve seams, leaving opening for pockets. Using crochet hook and D, make 8ch for button loop. Fasten off. Make 4 more loops, then sew to bodice and collar to fasten. Sew on toggles to correspond to button loops. Sew snaps in position to secure underflap.

Hat
Main part
Using No. 8 (5½mm) needles and C, cast on 73 sts. K 26 rows. Bind off.
Crown
Using No. 9 (6mm) needles and C, cast on 73 sts. K 3 rows.
Shape crown
1st dec row (K7, K2 tog) to last st, K1. 65 sts. K 1 row.
2nd dec row (K6, K2 tog) to last st., K1. 57 sts. K 1 row.
Cont to dec in this way, working one st less between each dec on every alternate row until 17 sts rem.
K 1 row.
Next row (K2 tog) to last st, K1.
Cut off yarn, thread through rem sts, gather up tightly and secure. Join seam.

To finish
Join back seam of main part, then sew crown to main part using a neat slip stitch.

Technique tip
Working blanket stitch

The outer edges of each square have been finished with blanket stitch. This not only neatens the outer edge, but also produces an unusual effect when the squares are joined together.

To work blanket stitch, thread a large-eyed needle with yarn. With the edge toward you and working from left to right, work a back stitch on the wrong side of the square to secure the yarn. Bring needle and yarn to right side and insert needle into fabric from front to back, about ½in (1cm) from lower edge.

Hold yarn below edge. Bring needle forward under lower edge and over the top of the yarn.

Pull needle through fabric and draw up yarn until it lies along the edge. Insert needle through fabric again from front to back, about ½in (1cm) to the right of the previous stitch.

Repeat this movement around the outer edge, working stitches ½in (1cm) apart. Fasten off yarn.

KNITTING

Shades of the 40s

We've made this perky little Fair Isle sweater in colors reminiscent of the 40s. Try softer colors if you prefer.

Sizes
To fit 30[32:34:36]in (76[83:87:92]cm) bust.
Length, 20[20½:21:21½]in (51[52.5: 53.5:55]cm).
Sleeve seam, 4in (10cm).

Note Directions for larger sizes are in brackets []; where there is only one set of figures it applies to all sizes.

Materials
7[7:9:9]oz (200[200:240:240]g) of a
  sport yarn in main color (A)
2oz (40g) in each of 3 contrasting
  colors (B, C and D)
1 pair each Nos. 3, 4 and 5 (3¼, 3¾
  and 4mm) needles

Gauge
22sts and 28 rows to 4in (10cm) on No. 5 (4mm) needles over stockinette st.

Back
Using No. 4 (3¾mm) needles and A, cast on 77[83:89:95] sts. Work 7 rows stockinette st, so ending with K row. K1 row to mark hemline. Beg with K row, work 8 more rows stockinette st. Change to No. 5 (4mm) needles. Cont in stockinette st, work 2 rows, then inc one st at each end of next and every foll 12th row until there are 91[97:103:109] sts. Cont straight until work measures 13½in (34.5cm) from hemline, ending with a P row. Place marker at each end of last row to denote beg of armholes. Work 4[6:10:12] rows. Joining on and cutting off colors as required, beg Fair Isle patt.
1st row K3A, (1B, 5A) to last 4 sts, 1B, 3A.
2nd row P2A, (1B, 1A, 1B, 3A) to last 5 sts, 1B, 1A, 1B, 2A.
3rd row K1A, (5B, 1A) to end.
4th row P (1B, 1C) to last st, 1B.
5th row K with C.
6th-9th rows Work 4th to first rows in this order.
10th row P with A.
11th row K1D, (5A, 1D) to end.

12th row P1A, 1D, 3A, (1D, 1A, 1D, 3A) to last 2 sts, 1D, 1A.
13th row K3D, 1A, (5D, 1A) to last 3 sts, 3D.
14th row P (1B, 1D) to last st, 1B.
15th row K with B.
16th-20th rows Work 14th to 10th rows in that order.
Rep first to 10th rows, using C instead of B and D instead of C. Rep 11th to 20th rows, using B instead of D and C instead of B. Working with A only, cont in stockinette st until work measures 6½[7:7½:8]in (16.5[18:19:20.5]cm) from markers; end with P row.

Shape shoulders
Bind off 8[8:8:9] sts at beg of next 6 rows and 5[7:9:9] sts at beg of foll 2 rows. Cut off yarn and leave rem 33[35:37:37] sts on a holder.

Front
Work as for back from * to *. Work in Fair Isle patt as for back until work measures 4½[5:5½:6]in (11.5[12.5:14: 15]cm) from markers; end with P row.

Shape neck
Next row K35[37:39:42], turn and leave rem sts on spare needle. Complete this side of neck first. Dec one st at beg of next and foll 5 alternate rows. 29[31:33: 36] sts. Cont straight until front is same length as back up to beg of shoulder; end at side edge.

Shape shoulder
Bind off 8[8:8:9] sts at beg of next and foll 2 alternate rows. Work 1 row. Bind off. Return to sts on spare needle. With RS facing place next 21[23:25:25] sts on holder, join yarn to next st and patt to end of row. Complete to match first side reversing shaping.

Sleeves (alike)
Using No. 4 (3¾mm) needles and A, cast on 58[64:70:76] sts. Work 7 rows stockinette st, so ending with K row, K1 row to mark hemline. Beg with K row, work 8 more rows stockinette st. Change

to No. 5 (4mm) needles and cont in stockinette st, inc one st at each end of next and every foll alternate row until there are 72[78:84:90] sts. Cont straight until work measures 4in (10cm) from hemline. Bind off.

Neckband
Join right shoulder seam. Using No. 3 (3¼mm) needles, A and with RS facing pick up and K17 sts from left front neck, K sts from holder, pick up and K17 sts from right front neck, then K back neck sts from holder. 88[92:96:96] sts. Work 7 rows K1, P1 ribbing. Bind off in ribbing.

To finish
Press work on WS with warm iron over dry cloth. Join left shoulder and neckband seam. Sew bound-off edge of sleeves to armholes between markers. Join side and sleeve seams. Turn up and hem lower edge and sleeves.

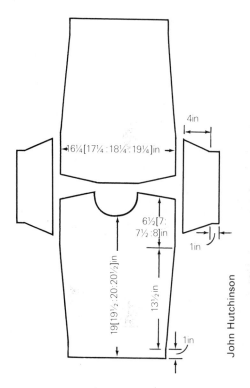

6¼[7¼:8¼:9¼]in

4in

6½[7: 7½:8]in

1in

19[19½:20:20½]in

13½in

1in

John Hutchinson

Gary Warren

Pretty pinafore

Fashion-conscious young ladies love this bib-topped skirt. The style is easily adaptable and the contrast fabric trimming is a pretty way to use up remnants.

Measurements
To fit ages 8, 10, 12. Waist to hem length: $19\frac{1}{2}[24\frac{1}{2}:25\frac{1}{2}]$in (50[62:65]cm). Waist: $19\frac{1}{2}[24\frac{1}{2}:25\frac{1}{2}]$in (50[62:65]cm)
Note Children's sizes vary considerably, so before cutting out check waist, skirt and strap lengths and adjust if necessary. $\frac{5}{8}$in (1.5cm) seam allowances have been included in measurement diagrams.

Materials
36in- (90cm-) wide fabric:
all ages: $1\frac{2}{3}$yd (1.5m)
54in- (140cm-) wide fabric:
age 8: $\frac{3}{4}$yd (.7m)
ages 10, 12: $1\frac{1}{2}$yd (1.4m)
$\frac{3}{4}$yd (.7m) of 36in- (90cm-) wide fabric in contrasting color
$\frac{1}{8}$yd (.1m) of 36in- (90cm-) wide interfacing
Matching thread, 5in (13cm) zipper,
Two $\frac{5}{8}$in (1.5cm) buttons
Two hooks and eyes
Tailor's chalk, yardstick

1 Mark and cut out all pattern pieces, following the diagrams on the right.

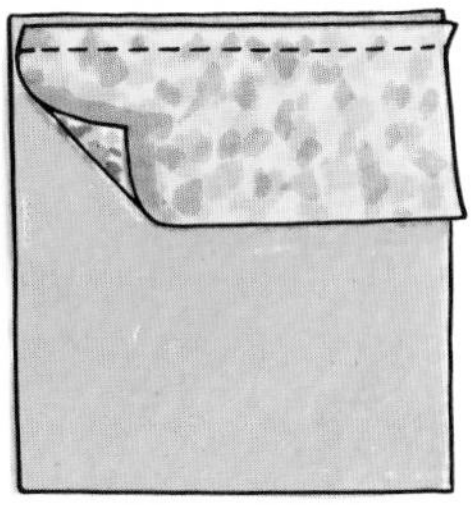

2 With right sides together, raw edges even, pin, baste and stitch pocket band to top of pocket. Trim seam allowance and press. Repeat for second pocket.

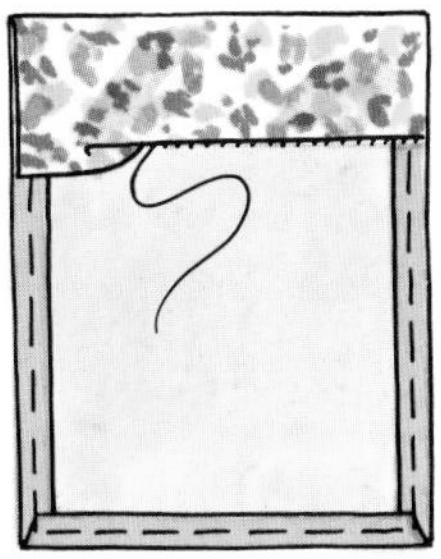

3 Turn under seam allowance on remaining long edge of pocket band and turn in short ends. Turn under seam

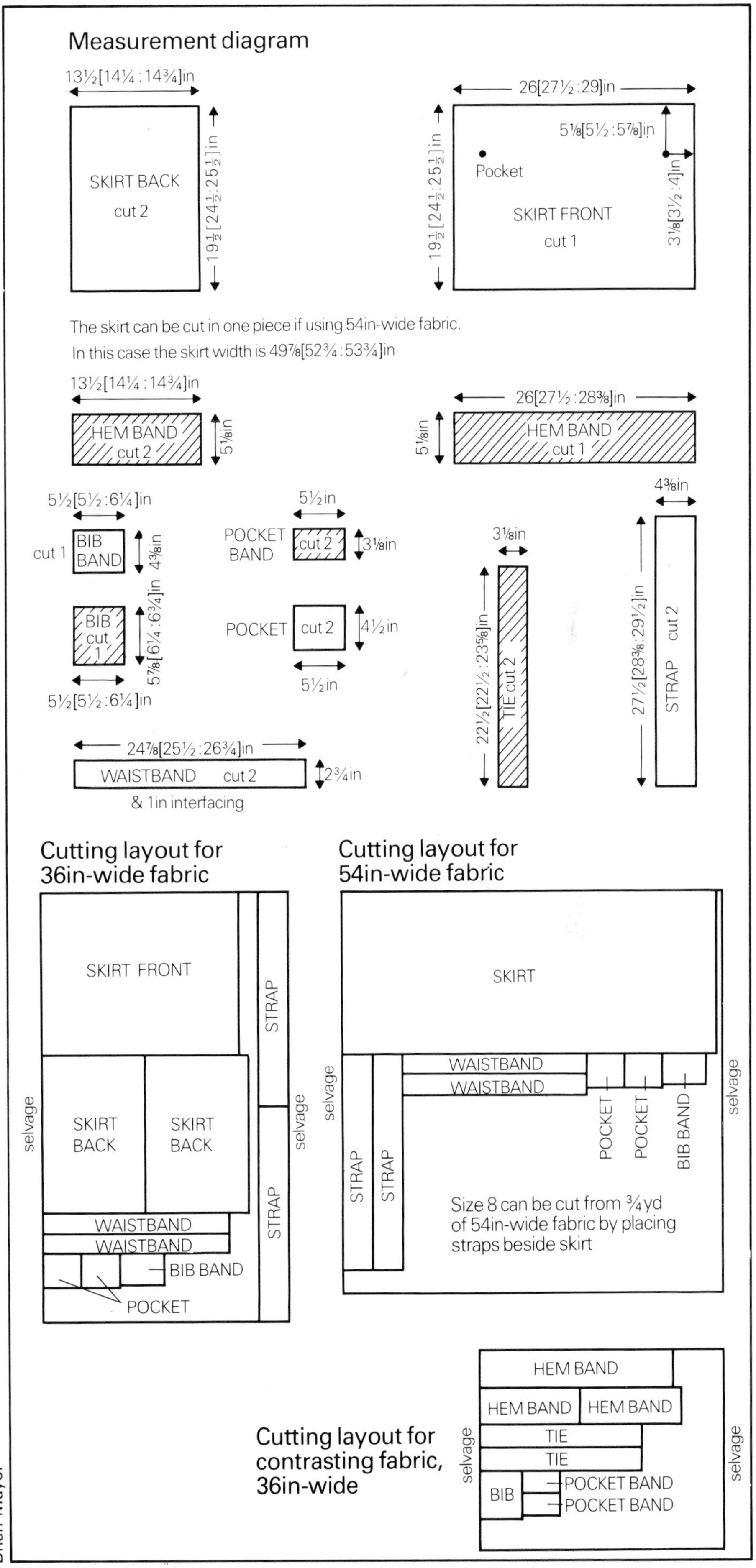

Measurement diagram
13½[14¼:14¾]in
SKIRT BACK
cut 2
19½[24½:25½]in
26[27½:29]in
5⅛[5½:5⅞]in
Pocket
SKIRT FRONT
cut 1
19½[24½:25½]in
3⅛[3½:4]in
The skirt can be cut in one piece if using 54in-wide fabric.
In this case the skirt width is 49⅞[52¾:53¾]in
13½[14¼:14¾]in
HEM BAND
cut 2
5⅛in
26[27½:28⅜]in
HEM BAND
cut 1
5⅛in
5½[5½:6¼]in
cut 1
BIB BAND
4⅜in
BIB
cut
1
5⅞[6¼:6¾]in
5½[5½:6¼]in
5½in
POCKET BAND
cut 2
3⅛in
POCKET
cut 2
4½in
5½in
3⅛in
TIE cut 2
22½[22½:23⅝]in
4⅜in
STRAP cut 2
27½[28⅜:29½]in
24⅞[25½:26¾]in
WAISTBAND cut 2
2¾in
& 1in interfacing
Cutting layout for 36in-wide fabric
SKIRT FRONT
STRAP
SKIRT BACK
SKIRT BACK
WAISTBAND
WAISTBAND
BIB BAND
POCKET
STRAP
selvage
selvage
Cutting layout for 54in-wide fabric
SKIRT
WAISTBAND
WAISTBAND
STRAP
STRAP
POCKET
POCKET
BIB BAND
Size 8 can be cut from ¾yd of 54in-wide fabric by placing straps beside skirt
selvage
selvage
Cutting layout for contrasting fabric, 36in-wide
HEM BAND
HEM BAND
HEM BAND
TIE
TIE
BIB
POCKET BAND
POCKET BAND
selvage
selvage

Brian Mayor

allowances on remainder of pocket, baste and press. Slip stitch free edges of pocket band. Repeat for second pocket, then keep to one side.

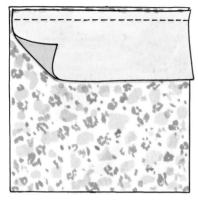

4 Stitch bib band to bib in the same way as pocket bands. Slip stitch free edge of bib band to inside of bib, as for pockets.

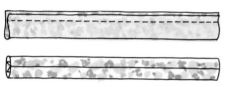

5 With right sides together, stitch long edge of tie. Trim seam allowance, turn right side out and press with seam in center of tie as shown. Repeat for second tie. Turn under seam allowance at both ends of each tie and slip stitch to finish.

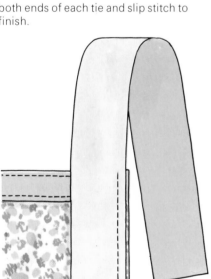

6 With right sides together and lower edges even, pin, baste and stitch one long edge of strap to bib edge. Turn under remainder of seam allowance along strap edge. Press seam allowances toward strap. Turn under seam allowances on opposite long edge and free end of strap. Press. Fold strap in half lengthwise, so that the folded edges meet.

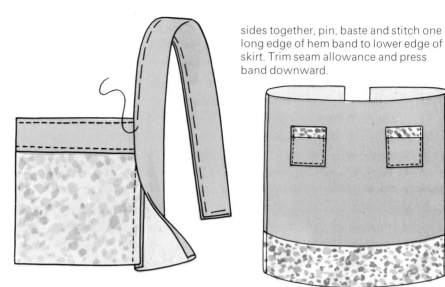

7 Pin, baste and topstitch down the length of the strap, across the end and up the other side. Repeat for second strap.

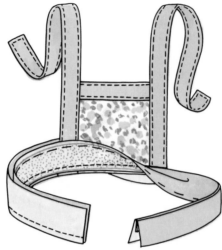

8 Baste interfacing to wrong side of one waistband. Matching centers of waistbands and bib, sandwich bib between right sides of waistband pieces with interfaced section on top. With raw edges even, pin, baste and stitch. Trim interfacing close to stitching line. Trim seam allowance, turn waistbands downward and press.

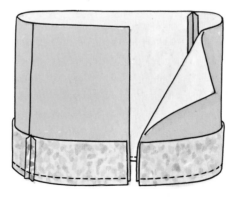

9 With right sides together stitch side seams, if necessary, and press. Stitch seams of hem band and press. With right

sides together, pin, baste and stitch one long edge of hem band to lower edge of skirt. Trim seam allowance and press band downward.

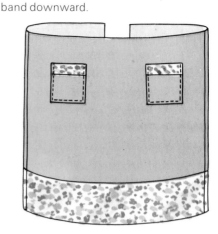

10 Working on right side of skirt, place outer corners of pockets at positions marked on measurement diagram. Pin, baste and topstitch close to edges of pockets.

11 With right sides together, stitch center back seam of skirt to within 5¾in (14.5cm) of waist, leaving an opening for the zipper. Press. Insert zipper in center back opening using slot seam method (see Volume 4, page 68).
Next, run two lines of gathering stitches within seam allowance around waist edge.
Pull up gathers to fit waistband, distributing fullness evenly.

Note At this stage it is advisable to try on the skirt to check for fit. It is quite easy to alter the length of the waistband, but bear in mind that there must be a little room to spare to fit a growing child. Since the hem is decorated with a fabric trim, it is necessary to make any adjustments to the length of the skirt at the waist edge. Check the length of the skirt before inserting the zipper.

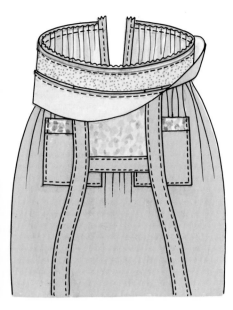

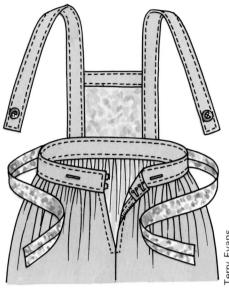

Terry Evans

12 With interfacing upward, matching centers, right sides together, pin and baste remaining long edge of waistband to skirt. Stitch with gathers facing upward. Trim seam allowances. Press waistband.
13 Turn under seam allowance on remaining long edge of waistband. Slip stitch edge of waistband over seamline on inside of skirt. Turn in ends of waistband and slip stitch. Topstitch close to upper edge of waistband.

14 Try skirt on child to establish correct positions for buttons and buttonholes, remembering that the straps cross over at the back. Work a buttonhole on each side of the center back opening and sew buttons to straps to correspond.
Sew on two hooks and eyes to finish waist opening.
Turn under seam allowance on lower edge of hem band and slip stitch over stitching line on wrong side of skirt.

Gary Warren

EXTRA SPECIAL SEWING

Casual comfort

These loosely cut pants have an elasticated waist and a tie at the front. Set pockets into the seams if you like, or add ties around the ankles for a harem look.

Measurements
To fit sizes 10 to 14 (the gathered waist makes these pants unsuitable for larger figures).
Finished length, waist to hem, 45in (114cm), plus 1⅝in (4cm) gathered top edge.
Seam allowances are ⅝in (1.5cm) throughout and a hem of 2in (5cm) is included.

Note Measurements are given for size 10; sizes 12 and 14 are given in brackets []; where only one figure is given this applies to all sizes.

Suggested fabrics
The pants should be made up in a solid-color fabric. A medium-weight poplin, light sailcloth or fine knit would be suitable.

Materials
3½yd (3.1m) of 36in (90cm)-wide fabric (all sizes) OR 1¾yd (1.6m) of 60in (150cm)-wide fabric (size 10 only); 3yd (2.7m) of 60in (150cm)-wide fabric (sizes 12 and 14)
1⅛yd (1m) of ⅝in (1.5cm)-wide matching seam binding
1⅛yd (1m) ¼in (6mm)-wide elastic
Dressmaker's graph paper (or shelf paper or brown paper)
Flexible curve, yardstick, thread

Note Although there are only two main pattern pieces, which can be cut directly from the fabric, you will find it easier to get an accurate result if you make a paper pattern first, following the appropriate measurements given for your size in the diagram. Check that the inner and outer pants seams are the same length on front and back pieces before cutting out the fabric. If you are taller than average, check the pants length and if necessary add extra length.

Gary Warren

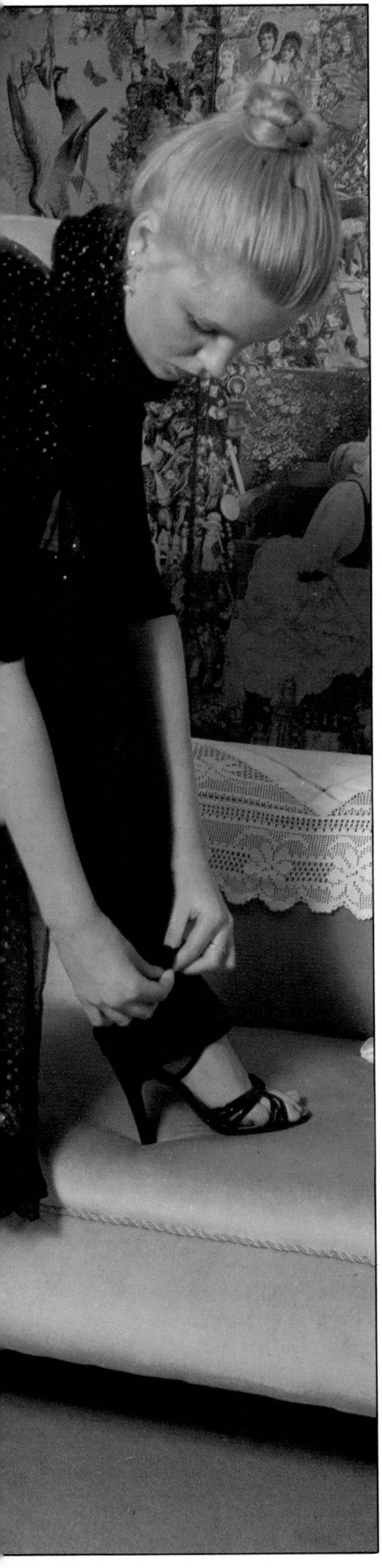

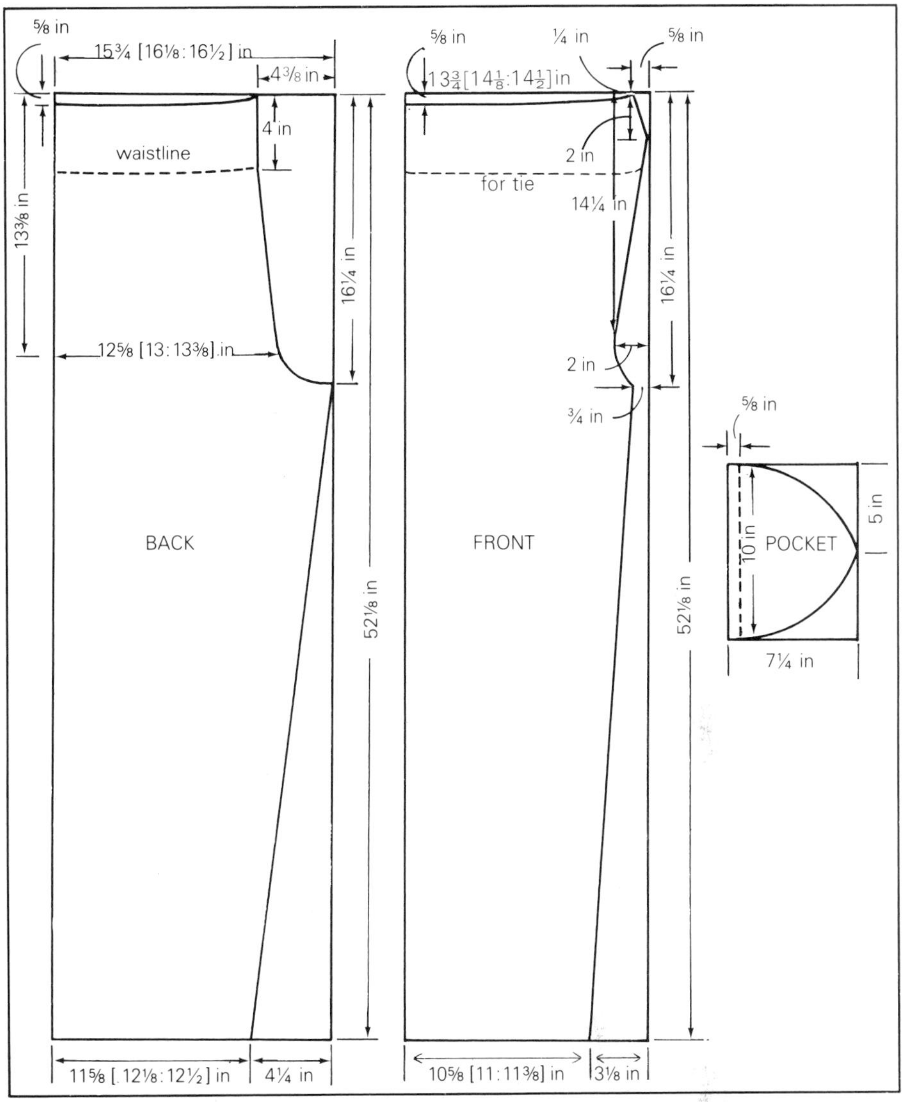

⅝ in
15¾ [16⅛:16½] in
4⅜ in
4 in
waistline
13⅜ in
12⅝ [13:13⅜] in
16¼ in
BACK
52⅛ in
11⅝ [12⅛:12½] in
4¼ in
⅝ in
¼ in
⅝ in
13¾[14⅛:14½]in
2 in
for tie
14¼ in
16¼ in
2 in
¾ in
FRONT
52⅛ in
10⅝ [11:11⅜] in
3⅛ in
⅝ in
10 in
POCKET
5 in
7¼ in

John Hutchinson

1 Cut out two front sections. Mark waistline with basting stitches 4in (10cm) from upper edge. Mark position for tie on each piece with a tailor's tack 6$\frac{3}{4}$in (17cm) from center front edge. Cut out two back sections and mark waistline as on front. For waist ties, cut two strips 1$\frac{1}{8}$in (3cm) by 17$\frac{3}{8}$in (44cm). For ankle ties (optional) cut out two strips each 2$\frac{3}{8}$in (6cm) by 23$\frac{5}{8}$in (60cm). Cut four pocket pieces (optional).

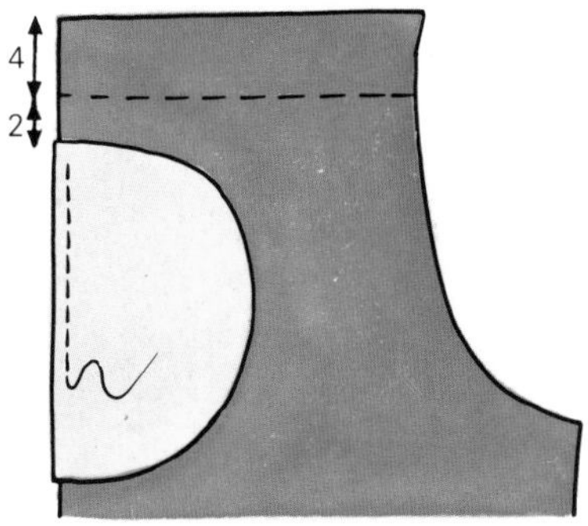

4
2

2 If you are making pockets, pin, baste and stitch one pocket piece to side seamline (long, straight edge) of front section, right sides together and raw edges even. Position the upper raw edge of the pocket 2in (5cm) down from the line of basting stitches at the waistline. Start stitching $\frac{5}{8}$in (1.5cm) from the top of the pocket and stitch down side seam for 6in (15.5cm) only. Leave remainder of pocket free at present.
Repeat for each pocket piece on side seamlines of remaining three sections.

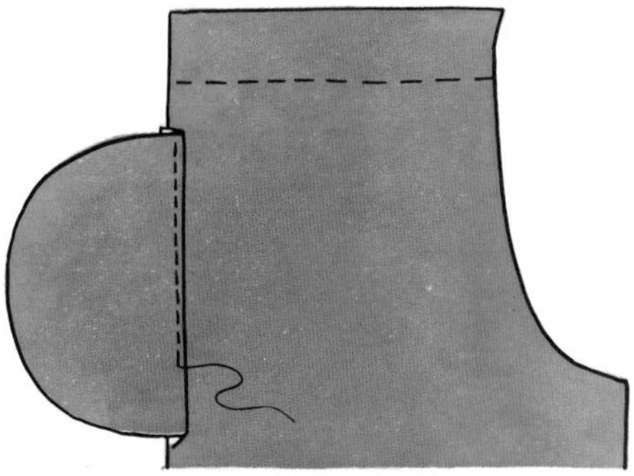

Terry Evans

3 Press pockets on back sections to one side. Topstitch each pocket to seam allowances $\frac{1}{8}$in (3mm) from seamline, 6in (15.5cm) down from upper seamline.

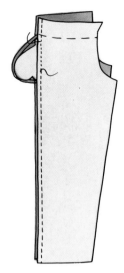

4 Pin, baste and stitch side seams, right sides together, leaving an opening for pockets if included. Press seams open and finish raw edges.

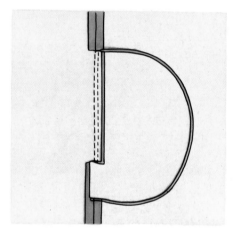

5 Clip the seam allowance of the back sections at top and bottom of pocket opening as shown. Clip seam allowances of pocket at bottom of seam.

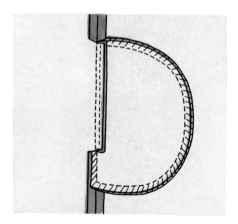

6 Pin, baste and stitch remaining edges of pocket. Sew raw edges together with zig-zag stitch or hand overcasting. Press pocket toward front. Topstitch upper pocket piece to front of pants, working from right side of pants, finishing off ends of thread neatly by hand.

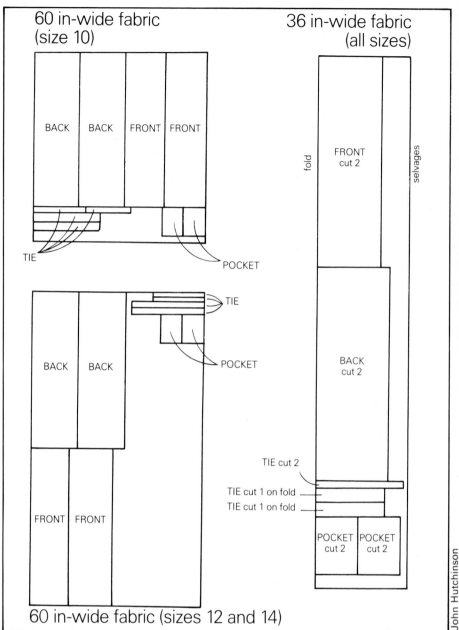

60 in-wide fabric (size 10)

BACK BACK FRONT FRONT

TIE

POCKET

36 in-wide fabric (all sizes)

fold

FRONT cut 2

selvages

BACK cut 2

TIE

POCKET

BACK BACK

FRONT FRONT

60 in-wide fabric (sizes 12 and 14)

TIE cut 2

TIE cut 1 on fold

TIE cut 1 on fold

POCKET cut 2   POCKET cut 2

John Hutchinson

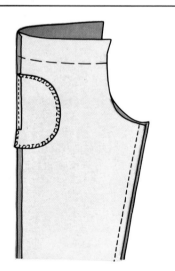

7 Pin, baste and stitch the inside leg seams with right sides together and raw edges even.

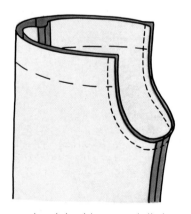

8 Turn one leg right side out and slip it inside the other leg. Pin, baste and stitch the curved crotch seam with right sides together, matching inside leg seams. Clip curves and press seam open. Finish edges with zig-zag stitch or overcasting. Turn pants right side out.

Terry Evans

9 Fold top of pants to inside so that the raw edge meets the line of basting stitches at the waistline. Baste raw edge in place temporarily and press folded edge.

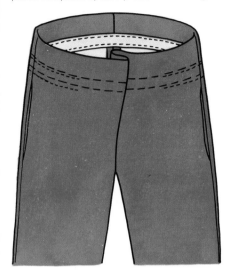

10 Fold in one end of seam binding $\frac{3}{8}$in (1cm) and, working on the wrong side, place the folded end of the seam binding at the tie position marked with a tailor's tack, centering it over the folded-under raw edge. Pin and baste the binding in place all around waistline until you reach the tailor's tack on the other front section. Allowing $\frac{3}{8}$in (1cm) for turning under, cut off seam binding. Stitch in place along both edges to form casing for elastic.

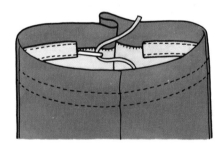

11 Insert elastic in casing using a safety pin or ball-point needle. Secure it at one end by stitching it firmly to pants front and casing, closing end of casing at the same time.

12 Try on pants, folding excess fabric at front to make a neat pleat. Pin in place temporarily. Pull up elastic so that pants fit comfortably at the waist. Mark the elastic to show the length needed. Also check that the leg length is correct. Cut off the elastic at the mark, and secure it at the other end of the casing.

13 Fold each waist tie piece in half lengthwise, right sides together. Stitch along length and across one short edge $\frac{3}{8}$in (1cm) from raw edges. Turn right side out. Press.
Make ankle ties in the same way, but finish the open edge on each tie by folding in seam allowance and slip stitching.

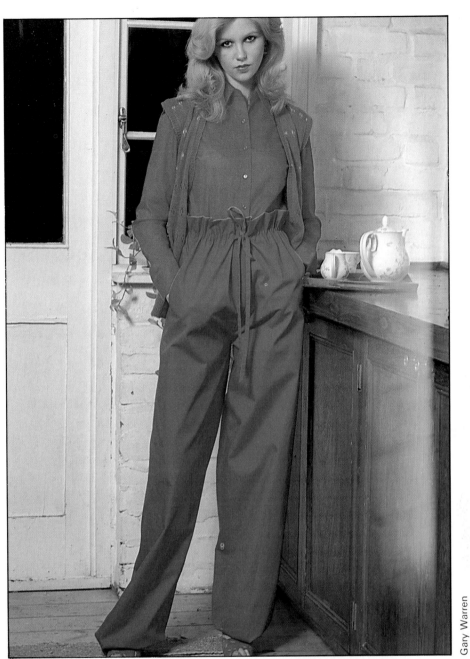

Gary Warren

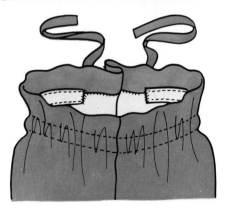

14 Pin and baste one waist tie to right side of pants front sections at each end of the elastic casing, folding under the raw edges. On the inside, overcast raw edge of waistline hem to pants between the ends of the casing.

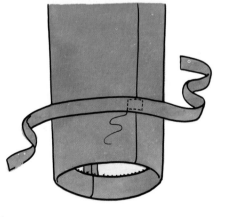

15 Turn up and hem legs. Attach ankle ties, if wanted, to legs. Match the center of each tie to the inside leg seam and stitch it in place neatly along the seamline.

Rainy day capers

This child's raincape will not only keep out the rain but will also act as a safety garment on gray days, if you make it in bright-colored fabric. We've chosen canary yellow nylon ciré and blue flannel, but you could make it in vinyl or wool if you prefer.

Measurements

To fit all ages 12 to 14. Measurements for age 14 given in brackets []. Directions are for a girl's cape. Reverse left and right front finishes for a boy.
Neck to hem length $30\frac{1}{4}[34\frac{1}{4}]$ in $(77[87]$cm$)$.
Neck to wrist length $24\frac{1}{4}[28\frac{1}{4}]$ in $(62[72]$cm$)$.

Note Check child's measurements before buying fabric. $\frac{5}{8}$ in (1.5cm) seam allowances are included.

Materials

60in (150cm)-wide fabric: $4[4\frac{3}{8}]$yd $(3.6[4]$m$)$
Matching thread
$1\frac{1}{8}$yd (1m) of 36in (90cm)-wide lightweight woven interfacing
Three $\frac{3}{4}$in (2cm) buttons
4in (10cm) of 1in (2.5cm)-wide seam binding
Tailor's chalk, yardstick
Flexible curve
Paperclips
Transparent tape

1 Place fabric on table or cutting board and, using tailor's chalk, a yardstick and a flexible curve, draw and cut out the right-hand side of the cape, following the cutting layout and the appropriate measurements shown on the diagram overleaf.

2 Using the right-hand side as a pattern, and placing right sides together, cut out the left-hand side of the cape, adding a $3\frac{1}{2}$in (9cm)-wide facing down the center front as shown in the diagram.
Cut out a buttonhole band, using the measurements shown. Mark the center front of the cape on both large sections with lines of basting $3\frac{1}{2}$in (9cm) from edge of left side of cape and $\frac{5}{8}$in (1.5cm) from edge of right side.

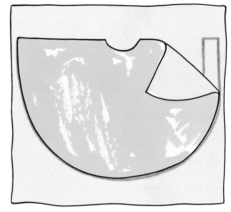

3 Next, cut out the facings. You will need two hem facings and two neck facings. Lay the hem of the RH section over some of the extra fabric and mark the curve of the hem with tailor's chalk, right sides together. Repeat for the LH hem facing and the neck facings, using the appropriate part of the sections you have cut out. Trim $3\frac{1}{2}$in (9cm) from the center front on the LH neck facing. For the wrist ties (optional) cut out four strips of fabric, $3\frac{1}{2}$in by $10\frac{1}{4}$in (9cm by 26cm).

4 Cut each neck facing piece again from interfacing.
Cut a strip of interfacing 2in (5cm) wide and same length as front facing. Cut a strip of interfacing $1\frac{1}{8}$in (3cm) wide and same length as buttonhole band.

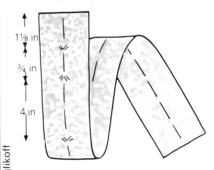

$1\frac{1}{8}$ in

$\frac{3}{4}$ in

4 in

5 Make a line of basting stitches down center front of the interfacing strip of buttonhole band. Then mark positions of each buttonhole with two tailor's tacks,

Serge Krouglikoff

Terry Evans

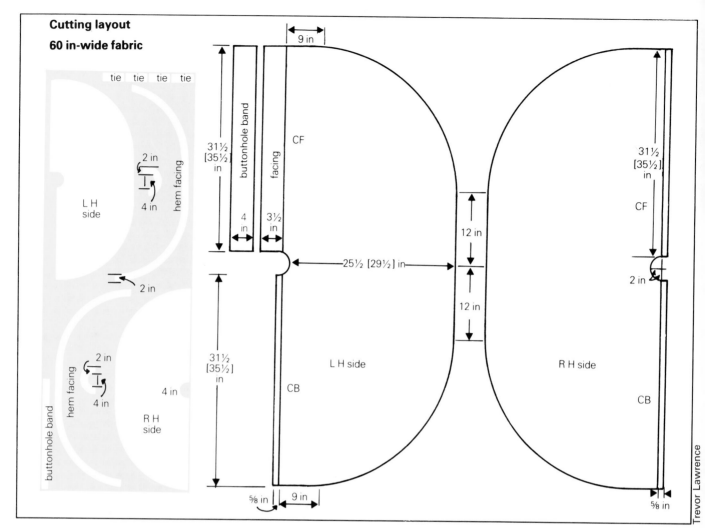

Cutting layout

60 in-wide fabric

tie tie tie tie

L H side

hem facing

2 in
4 in

2 in

hem facing

2 in
4 in

R H side

4 in

buttonhole band

buttonhole band

facing

CF

31½ [35½] in

4 in

3½ in

25½ [29½] in

L H side

CB

5⁄8 in   9 in

CF

31½ [35½] in

CF

12 in

12 in

R H side

CB

2 in

31½ [35½] in

5⁄8 in

Trevor Lawrence

as follows: measure down 1⅛in (3cm) from top of band and make a pair of tailor's tacks ¾in (2cm) apart, then measure down 4in (10cm) again and make another pair of tacks ¾in (2cm) apart. Repeat to mark position of third buttonhole.

6 Stitch the left side of the cape to right side down center back, using a flat felled seam. Join the two neck facing pieces, the neck interfacings and the two hem facing pieces in the same way. Baste neck interfacing to wrong side of facing and finish outer edge by turning under and hemming.

7 Sew interfaced neck facings to cape along neck edge, with right sides together and raw edges even. Start stitching 1⅛in (3cm) from right front edge. On the LH side, finish stitching 1⅛-1⅝in (3-4cm) from center front line. Trim seam allowances around neck edge. Clip into seam allowances around curve of seam. Turn facing to inside. Topstitch around stitched part of neck edge, 1⅛in (3cm) from seam, to help the facing lie flat.

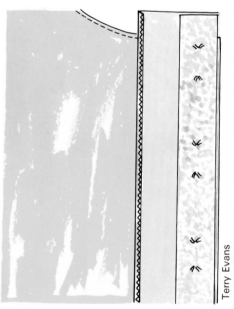

Terry Evans

8 Finish one long edge of the buttonhole band by folding ¼in (6mm) to the wrong side and finishing with zig-zag stitch. Position unfinished center front edge of buttonhole band on center front edge of right-hand section of cape. The upper, short end of the band should extend 5⁄8in (1.5cm) above the faced neck edge.

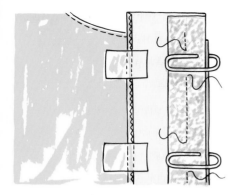

9 Position interfacing on top of buttonhole band and use paperclips and transparent tape to hold the three pieces of fabric in place. Stitch down the center line of basting, stopping at each of the marked points. Leave threads long enough to tie off by hand. After stitching the two 4in (10cm) sections between the buttonholes, stitch straight down to hem.

10 Remove basting threads and sew in thread ends at buttonholes by hand. Open seam allowance and finger press so that it lies flat. Finish seam allowance of main section.

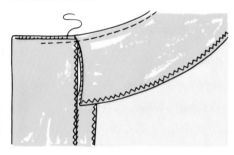

11 On wrong side, turn back free edge of buttonhole band and slip stitch the finished edge in place alongside the seam joining the band to the cape, just clearing the buttonholes. Fold in and slip stitch the seam allowance of the buttonhole band across the upper edge. Fold under the seam allowance of the short edge of the neck facing and slip stitch to seam allowance down center front of main cape. Continue the line of topstitching around the neck edge to the center front and sew in thread ends.

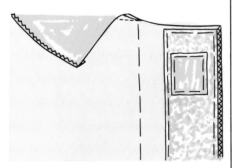

12 On the left half of the cape, finish edge of center front facing by folding in ¼in (6mm) and zig-zag stitching. Baste

interfacing to wrong side of facing, matching one edge to the folded-in edge of the facing and positioning the other edge 1in (2.5cm) from the center front line. Mark the button positions to correspond with the buttonholes and baste a 1in (2.5cm) square of interfacing over each position to reinforce it.

13 Fold the facing along the edge of the interfacing. (The center front line should lie over the center of the interfacing.) Topstitch finished edge to main part of cape.

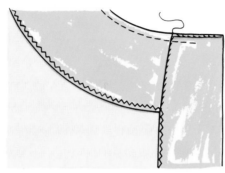

14 Turn in seam allowance at top of facing and slip stitch in place. Trim the short, unfinished edge of the neck facing, turn under and slip stitch it to the front facing. Finish topstitching as described for right-hand side in step 11.

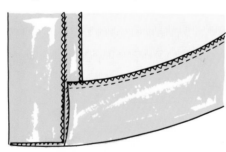

15 Finish the inner curved edge of the hem facing by turning it under and zig-zag stitching. Stitch hem facing around hem, with right sides together and

raw edges even. Turn the facing to the inside and topstitch close to the zig-zagged edge. Finish the lower ends of the buttonhole band and front facing by turning in and slip stitching. Turn under and slip stitch short, raw edges of hem facing to buttonhole band and front facing.

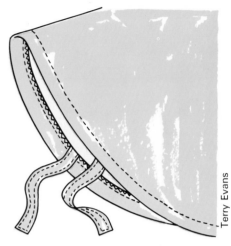

Terry Evans

16 For ties (optional) fold each strip in half lengthwise with right sides together. Stitch each short end and all but 2in (5cm) of the long edge. Turn ties right side out. Slip stitch along opening. Topstitch all around tie, ¼in (6mm) from edges, to give a firm finish. Topstitch each pair of ties to cape near hem edge, placing each tie 8in (20cm) from the center wrist point.

17 Sew on buttons to correspond with buttonholes.

Serge Krouglikoff

Technique tip

Working with nylon ciré

Use fine hand and machine needles and polyester thread.

The right side of nylon ciré is shiny and the wrong side is matt. Be careful not to confuse them.

Avoid pinning whenever possible, as pins leave tiny holes in the fabric. Instead, hold fabric with paperclips and transparent tape, which can be stitched through and then peeled away. Keep the basting to a minimum for the same reasons. Unavoidable basting stitches should be made inside the seam allowances.

DO NOT PRESS the fabric—this will make it curl. Instead, flatten seams with fingertips. The raw edges of this fabric ravel quickly, so try to finish seam edges as soon as possible after cutting out the fabric. Finish seam allowances with narrow ⅛in (3mm) hems, either straight or zig-zag stitched.

Main body seams can be flat felled for a practical, readymade finish.

Cherry blossom time

The simplest meal will become a little more festive when you use this charming tablecloth. Three simple stitches are all you need for the cherry blossom design.

Materials
- *Plain white cotton or fine linen table-cloth, 52 x 52in (132 x 132cm); you could also use a circular, oblong or oval cloth or make a cloth to fit your table*
- *6 skeins stranded embroidery floss in salmon pink; 1 skein each in pale blue; yellow-orange; brown; and sage green*
- *Crewel needle, size 6*
- *Tracing paper*
- *Dressmaker's carbon paper*
- *Wooden embroidery hoop, about 8in (20.5cm) in diameter*

1 Trace the cherry blossom design on a sheet of tracing paper.

Jerry Tubby

Terry Evans

2 Transfer the design to each corner of the tablecloth, using a piece of dressmaker's carbon paper slightly smaller than the tracing paper. Lay the carbon paper on the cloth at one corner and lay the

Terri Lawlor

tracing on top of it, checking that the motif is positioned centrally across the corner as shown on the diagram. Pin the corners of the tracing paper to the cloth. Trace over the design with a pencil. Repeat for the other three corners.

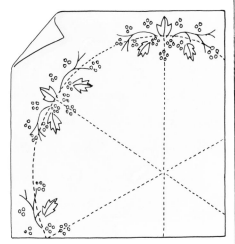

3 On another sheet of tracing paper, draw a circle about 17¾in (45cm) in diameter and mark the center. Divide the circle into six equal segments. Center the line and arc of the circle for each segment over the blossom design and trace it. You should end up with a wreath of blossoms evenly spaced around your circle.
4 Find the center of the cloth by folding it crosswise and then lengthwise and marking the point where the folds intersect with a pin.
5 Matching the center of the circle to the center of the cloth, transfer the design to the tablecloth, using dressmaker's carbon, in the same way as you did the corner motifs.

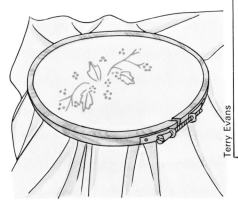

6 Make sure your embroidery hoop is clean, so that it will not leave a mark on the fabric. Place one corner of the cloth over the inside ring and push the outer ring over it. Adjust the screw on the ring to make sure the fabric is taut. Following the stitch and color guide, complete all embroidery within the area of the hoop.

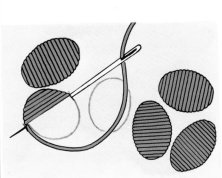

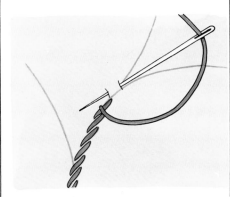

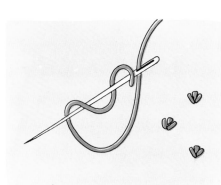

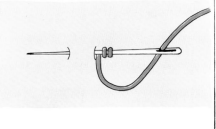

Terry Evans

7 First embroider the petals. Thread the needle with three strands of embroidery floss in salmon ; knot the end. Bring the needle up to the right side at the edge of one petal. Work straight stitches close together across the shape, making sure the transfer line is covered and the edges neat. Fill in all the petals within the hoop in the same way. Note that the direction of the stitches varies from petal to petal on each flower.

8 Thread the needle with three strands of brown and outline the stems within the hoop area using stem stitch. Work from left to right on the design with small overlapping stitches as shown. Re-thread needle with three strands of green, and using the same stitch, outline the leaves.
9 Thread the needle with three strands of blue and embroider French knots where shown on the design. To make a French knot, bring thread through from the back of the cloth at the required position. Holding thread down with your left thumb, wind needle around it twice as shown in the drawing. Still holding thread tight, twist needle around to starting point and reinsert it close to the point where the thread emerged. Pull thread through to back and secure to complete a knot or insert it at the point where a nearby knot is to be made.
10 Using three strands of yellow-orange work the remaining French knots. Move the hoop to another corner of the cloth and complete the design there in the same way.
11 After finishing the corners, move the hoop to the center and embroider the wreath design, moving the embroidery frame around the circle as you complete each section.
12 When all the embroidery is completed, press the tablecloth on the wrong side with a steam iron or use a dry iron with a damp cloth, first placing it over a folded bath towel. The spongy layer underneath will help to make the stitches stand out against the cloth.

Homemaker

Orderly papers

This writing case will help you to keep your desk in order. It will hold all those bits and pieces that you need to write the letter that someone, somewhere is expecting.

S. Wells

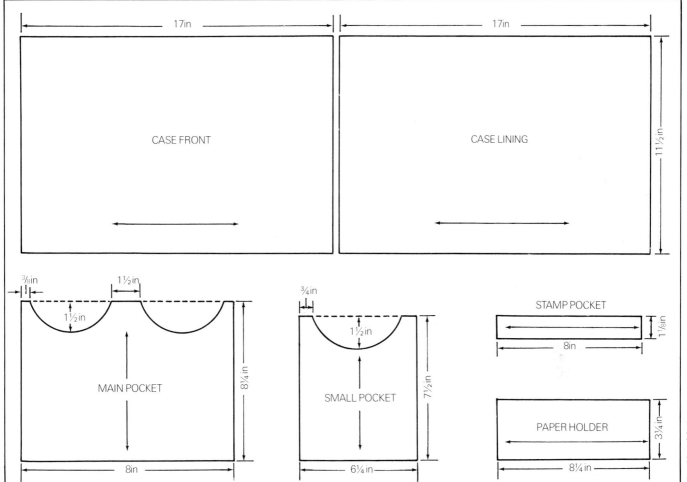

CASE FRONT

17in

CASE LINING

17in

11½in

³⁄₈in 1½in

1½in

MAIN POCKET

8¼in

8in

¾in

1½in

SMALL POCKET

7½in

6¼in

STAMP POCKET

1⅛in

8in

PAPER HOLDER

3¼in

8¼in

Materials
¾yd (.6m) of 36in (90cm)-wide
   patterned fabric
2⅜yd (2.1m) of matching bias binding
12×18in (30×45cm) rectangle of
   lightweight batting
Sewing thread
15½×10in (40×25cm) cardboard

1 Cut out the six pieces for the case from the patterned fabric.

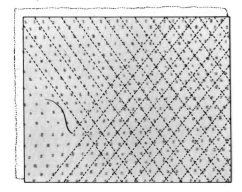

2 Baste the rectangle of batting to the wrong side of the fabric for the case front. Stitch lines of quilting diagonally across the fabric, spacing them at 1in (2.5cm) intervals. Stitch lines of quilting diagonally across the fabric in the

opposite direction also spaced at 1in (2.5cm) intervals, so that you form a diamond pattern.

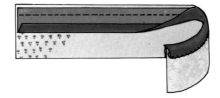

3 Baste and stitch bias binding to one long edge of the piece for the stamp pocket, placing binding and fabric with right sides together and raw edges matching, and stitching on the fold of the binding. Press the binding over to the wrong side, turn under free edge, and slipstitch down close to the machine stitching.

4 Baste the stamp pocket piece to the bottom (short) edge of the main pocket with raw edges together and both right sides facing upward. Stitch the pocket in place with two lines of vertical stitching, the first 3in (7.5cm) from the left-hand side, and the second 2½in (6.5cm) to the right of the first row. Trim away the right-hand corner of the stamp pocket where it overlaps the curved edge of the main pocket.

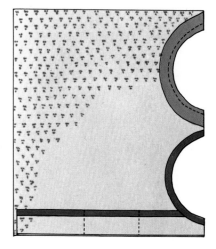

5 Bind the two curves of the main pocket piece in the same way as the stamp pockets, covering the cut-away corner of the stamp pocket at the same time. Bind the curved edge of the small pocket in the same way.

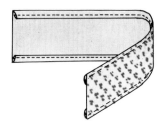

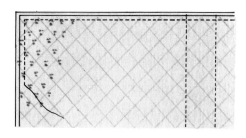

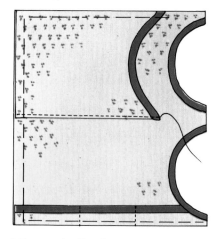

6 Turn under $\frac{3}{8}$in (1cm) along the lower (long) edge of the small pocket; press. Baste the small pocket to the top of the main pocket, matching raw edges at top and side. Baste and stitch small pocket to main pocket along turned-under edge, stitching close to the fold.

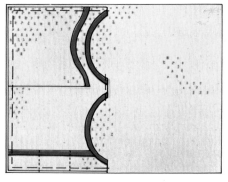

7 Turn under $\frac{3}{8}$in (1cm) along the small straight edge between curves of main pocket; press. Baste the main pocket to the left-hand side of the case lining with right sides facing and raw edges matching.

8 Baste and stitch $\frac{1}{4}$in (6mm) double hems on both long edges of the paper holder. Turn under $\frac{3}{8}$in (1cm) along the left-hand edge and trim corners. Baste ends of paper holder to case lining, positioning it as shown. It should be $1\frac{1}{2}$in (4cm) from the top, raw edge of the case, and there should be a clear strip 1in (2.5cm) wide down the center of the lining, which will form the spine of the case.

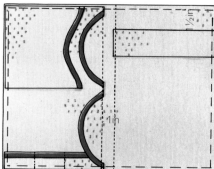

9 Baste the case lining to the case front with wrong sides facing. Stitch from top to bottom of the case, 8in (20cm) from the left-hand side, through both layers. This will secure the straight edge at the center of the main pocket, above and below curves. Add another line of stitching parallel to the first and 1in (2.5cm) to the right. This will secure the paper holder.

10 Stitch around the outer edge of the case taking $\frac{3}{8}$in (1cm) seams but leaving the bottom edge open.

11 Cut the cardboard into three pieces: two pieces measuring $10 \times 7\frac{1}{4}$in (25 × 18.5cm) and one piece measuring 10 × $\frac{7}{8}$in (25 × 2.3cm). Insert the cardboard pieces between the case front and lining through lower opening. Stitch opening.

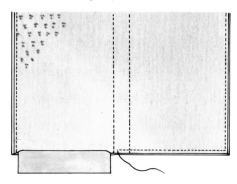

12 Baste and stitch binding to the lining of the case all around, following the previous line of stitching and turning under short ends for a neat joining. Slip stitch the binding in place on the quilted outside of case, working the stitches as close as possible to the previous line of stitching.

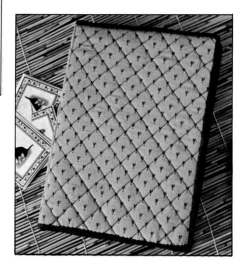

Homemaker

Sail set

Make something special of a baby's plain sleeper by adding a collar, "shoes" and bib with an appliquéd boat.

Materials

Baby's terry cloth sleeper
½yd (.4m) of 36in (90cm)-wide print fabric
⅜yd (.3m) of 36in (90cm)-wide stretch terry cloth to match suit
⅜yd (.3m) of 36in (90cm)-wide white cotton fabric for backing bib
⅜yd (.3m) of 36in (90cm)-wide lightweight polyester batting
2yd (1.8m) of contrasting bias binding
¾yd (.7m) of ⅜in (1cm)-wide lace edging
Matching thread
1 skein of stranded embroidery floss in a color similar to bias binding
2 small buttons
Sheets of tracing paper for patterns
Dressmaker's carbon paper
Embroidery hoop (optional)

Bib

1 Cut out 9in (23cm) squares from the print fabric, terry cloth, white cotton backing and batting.
2 Using the tracing paper, trace and cut out the pattern given for the bib. Transfer the boat design onto the right side of the print fabric, using the dressmaker's carbon and tracing paper.

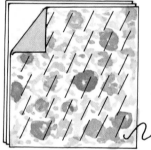

3 Place the batting between the printed fabric and the cotton backing, with the right sides of these fabrics facing outward. Carefully baste the layers together, working large stitches from the center of the square out to each side. This basting will prevent the layers from slipping out of place when you do the quilting embroidery.

4 Using all six strands of embroidery floss work the boat design in a chain stitch. You can work the embroidery with the fabric held in your hand or use an embroidery hoop to hold the fabric taut. Press the quilting lightly by using a pressing cloth.

BIB

cut around solid line when quilted embroidery is complete

sewing line   ▬ ▬ ▬ ▬

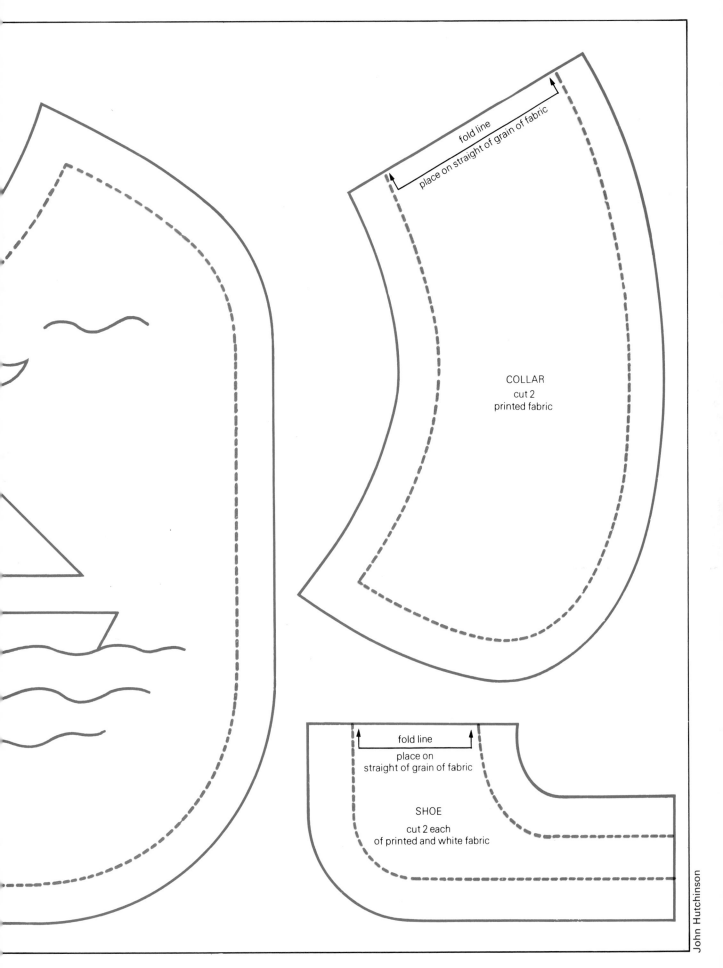

fold line
place on straight of grain of fabric

COLLAR
cut 2
printed fabric

fold line
place on
straight of grain of fabric

SHOE

cut 2 each
of printed and white fabric

John Hutchinson

5 Baste the square of terry cloth to the back of the quilted bib, working the decorative basting stitches close to the embroidery, as shown. Pin the paper pattern for the bib over the quilting, aligning the design tracing with the chain stitch already embroidered. Trim away the excess fabric outside the pattern piece.

6 Baste and stitch the bias binding to the front of the bib along the sides and lower edge, aligning the raw edges and stitching on the foldline of the binding. Slip stitch the binding to the line of machine stitching on the wrong side.

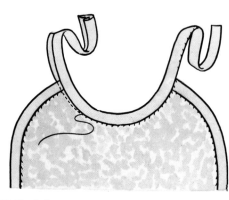

7 Bind the neck edge in the same way, but leave 5in (13cm) of binding at each end of the neck for ties. Fold the binding to the wrong side and fold each tie piece in half. Slip stitch from the end of one tie around neck to end of other tie.

Collar

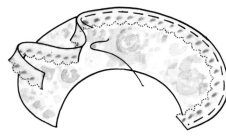

1 Trace the paper pattern for the collar and check that it fits your suit. Make any necessary adjustments and cut out two collar pieces from the print fabric. Baste the lace around the outer edge of one collar piece on the right side, $\frac{3}{8}$in (1cm) from raw edge. The decorative edge of the lace should face inward.
2 Pin the two collar pieces together with right sides facing. Stitch the two pieces together $\frac{3}{8}$in (1cm) from the raw edge, leaving the neck edge unstitched. Trim and clip the curved edges and turn the collar right side out. Press. Bind the back edge in the same way as the bib.

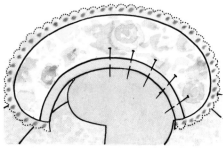

3 Matching the center back of the suit neck to the center of the collar, pin collar to the inside of the suit neck, working from the center around to each front. Hand sew the collar in place so it can be removed and attached to another suit if necessary.

Shoes

1 Trace the pattern for the shoe pieces and check that they fit the feet of your suit. Make any necessary adjustments and cut out two shoe pieces in both the printed fabric and the white cotton. backing.

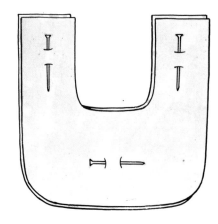

2 Stitch one printed fabric shoe to one white cotton shoe, right sides facing, taking $\frac{3}{8}$in (1cm) seams. Leave the two ends unstitched. Trim seams, clip seam allowances and turn the shoes right side out.

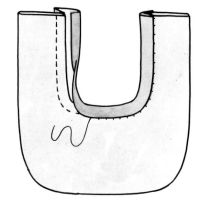

3 Bind the inner curved edge of the shoe in the same way as the bib.

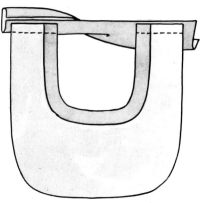

4 Cut a strip of binding to fit right across the shoe to form a bar, allowing small hems on each end. Place the binding across the upper edges of the shoe, as shown. Baste in place. Fold the binding in half and tuck in the raw ends. Press. Hand sew the binding folds together in the middle and sew the remaining edges to wrong side of shoe.

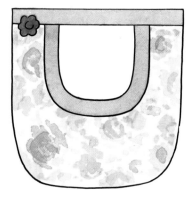

5 Attach a small button to the outer side of the shoe. Pin and neatly hand sew the shoe to the foot of the suit along the side and toe ends. Make and attach the other shoe in the same way.

Terry Evans

Homemaker

Sheet magic

A dye bath and some coordinating printed fabric are all you need to transform a plain old double sheet into a decorative single sheet and matching pillow case.

Materials
1 double sheet 90 x 104in
  (229 x 264cm)
Fabric dye (if using a white sheet)
1⅛yd (1m) of 36in (90cm)-wide
  printed cotton fabric
Matching sewing thread

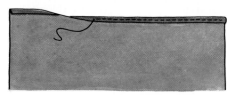

1 If using a white sheet, dye it the required color, following the directions on the package. Allow the sheet to dry and press it. If the sheet is already colored, simply press it. Cut a rectangle measuring 69½ x 104in (177 x 264cm) (the remaining piece will be used to make the pillowcase). Turn under a ⅛in (2mm) hem; press. Turn under a further ¼in (5mm) to make a double hem on one long side. Repeat for the other side. Pin and baste in place. Stitch, using a small straight stitch close to the edge.

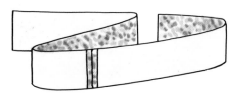

2 To make the trim, cut two strips widthwise from the printed cotton, each measuring 36 x 8in (90 x 22cm). Pin, baste and stitch the short ends together, taking ¼in (5mm) seams, to make one strip 71½in (179cm) long.

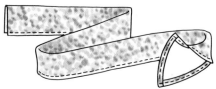

3 Turn under a ¼in (5mm) hem on all four edges of the printed fabric. Press and baste in place. Machine stitch close to the edge. With wrong sides together, fold the strip in half lengthwise and press along the fold.

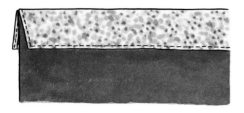

4 Position the strip over the upper edge of the sheet, making sure that the sheet edge fits smoothly between the two layers of the printed strip. Make sure that you have an equal amount of printed fabric on both sides of the sheet.

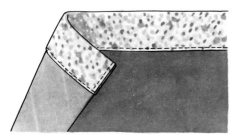

5 Pin and baste the strip in position. Machine stitch all around the trim, $\frac{1}{8}$in (3mm) from the edge. Press on both sides.
6 From the remaining sheet fabric cut out two rectangles, each measuring 20 x 29in (50 x 74cm), to form the two sides of the pillowcase, and another rectangle measuring 20 x 8$\frac{3}{4}$in (50 x 22cm), to form the pillowcase pocket.
On one large rectangle turn under $\frac{1}{8}$in (2mm) along one short edge and press. Turn under a further $\frac{1}{4}$in (5mm) to form a double hem. Pin, baste and stitch close to the edge. This will form the opening edge of the pillowcase and is now the upper side of the pillowcase.

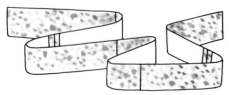

7 For the ruffle, cut the remaining cotton print widthwise into six 3in (8cm)-wide strips. Pin, baste and stitch the short ends together, taking $\frac{1}{4}$in (5mm) seams, to make one long strip. Trim the strip to measure 180in (457cm) in length.

8 Turn under $\frac{1}{8}$in (2mm) along one long edge of the strip and press. Turn under a further $\frac{1}{4}$in (5mm) to form a double hem. Pin, baste and stitch close to the edge, using a straight stitch.

Run two lines of gathering along the other long edge of the strip. Pull up gathering threads to fit around pillowcase edge.

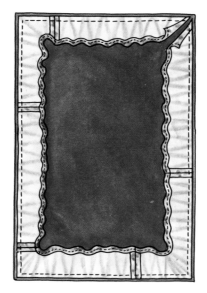

9 Pin and baste the gathered ruffle to the right side of the lower pillowcase piece, with the ungathered edge inward, the wrong side of ruffle upward, and the two short ends meeting with two $\frac{1}{4}$in (5mm) seam allowances kept free.

10 Place the upper pillowcase piece on the trimmed lower piece, right sides together, and all raw edges even. Baste around edges, making sure that the ruffle gathers are not caught up in the basting. Stitch all around close to the edge, leaving finished edge at top free. Turn under $\frac{1}{4}$in (5mm) on the two short ends of the ruffle and slip stitch these edges together.

11 Turn under $\frac{1}{8}$in (2mm) along one long edge of the pillowcase pocket piece. Press. Turn under a further $\frac{1}{4}$in (5mm) to form a double hem. Pin, baste and stitch close to the edge. Position the right side of the pocket to the wrong side of the upper pillowcase piece, with all raw edges even. Pin, baste and stitch the pocket piece to the pillowcase along the three raw edges, taking care, as you stitch along the short edge of the case, to *pull the upper piece out of the way of the stitching.* Trim seams and finish with machine zig-zagging or hand overcasting.

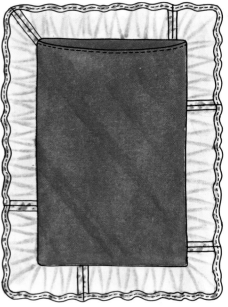

12 Turn pillowcase right side out and press.

Homemaker

For romantics at heart

These lovely pillows are made in soft pastel fabrics with lots of lace. Make one or make them all, and bring a little romance into your life.

Gary Warren

Large rectangular pillow

Size
18 × 27½in (45 × 70cm).

Materials
White pillow form measuring 18 ×
27½in (45 × 70cm)
$\frac{5}{8}$*yd (·5m) of 36in (90cm) wide white*
eyelet lace fabric
$\frac{5}{8}$*yd (·5m) of 36in (90cm) wide plain*
cotton fabric in white or green
3$\frac{7}{8}$*yd (3.5m) of 2$\frac{3}{4}$in (7cm)*
green and white eyelet lace edging
2$\frac{3}{4}$*yd (2.5m) of $\frac{3}{4}$in (2cm) wide white*
eyelet lace insertion
1$\frac{7}{8}$*yd (1.7m) of $\frac{3}{4}$in (2cm) wide apple*
green satin ribbon, cut into two 20in
(50cm) lengths and two 14in
(35cm) lengths
3$\frac{5}{8}$*yd (3.3m) of $\frac{3}{8}$in (1cm) wide dark*
green satin ribbon
$\frac{5}{8}$*yd (.5m) each of two different $\frac{3}{8}$in*
(1cm) wide white lace edgings, or
1$\frac{1}{8}$*yd (1m) of the same lace*
$\frac{5}{8}$*yd (.5m) each of two different $\frac{3}{4}$in*
(2cm) wide eyelet lace edgings, or
1$\frac{1}{8}$*yd (1m) of the same edging*
2 small lace flower motifs
Sewing thread in white, apple green
and dark green

1 Cut out a rectangle measuring 20 × 29½in (50 × 75cm) from the eyelet lace fabric and another of the same size from the plain cotton fabric. Press 1in (2.5cm) to the wrong side all around both pieces. Put one piece aside for the back section.

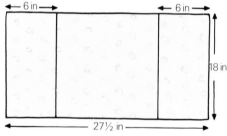

2 Add a line of basting across the eyelet lace panel which is 6in (16cm) in from the short edges at both sides of the rectangle.

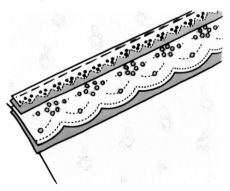

3 Pin the ribbon and the lace across the lines marked on the panel. Position the outer edge of the 20in (50cm) length of apple green ribbon against each of these lines. Overlap the ribbon slightly with the $\frac{3}{4}$in (2cm) wide eyelet lace edging, so the two edges are together, using either two pieces of the same lace or a different type at each side. Overlap the raw edges of the eyelet lace edging with 20in (50cm) of the dark green ribbon on each side and position the white lace edging over this, using either the same edging on both sides or a different type of edging on each side.
Pin the layers of lace and ribbon in place across the panel and baste. Sew them in place by hand or machine.
Press under the ends of ribbon and lace trimming along the lines already pressed in the edges of the front panel.

4 Tie the remaining pieces of apple green ribbon in bows. Position the lace flower motifs on the front of the fabric, then center a bow on each and hand-sew in place.

5 Now prepare the green and white eyelet lace to apply around the edge of the front panel.
Join ends of the green and white eyelet lace and run a gathering thread close to the raw edge.
Now draw up the gathers to fit the outer edge of the front section and baste the lace to the pillow front as shown, aligning the raw edges of the lace and of the fabric.

6 The next step is to join the trimmed front section to the plain back section.
Place the front section over the plain back section, wrong sides together, aligning the turned-under edges of the fabric. Baste and machine stitch close to the edge, leaving one end open for inserting the pillow form.

7 Thread the narrow green ribbon through the insertion lace and pin the outer edge of the lace to the front section, covering the seamline, starting from one corner. Stitch in place. Catch the insertion lace to the eyelet lace fabric along the inner edge.
Insert the pillow and sew up the opening invisibly.

Square pillow

Size
14in (35cm) square.

Materials
White pillow form 14in (35cm) square
$\frac{5}{8}$*yd (.6m) of 36in (90cm) wide green*
print fabric
13in (33cm) square of white eyelet lace
fabric
2$\frac{1}{4}$*yd (2m) of 3in (8cm) wide eyelet*
lace edging
1$\frac{3}{4}$*yd (1.6m) of $\frac{3}{4}$in (2cm) wide*
pointed white eyelet lace edging
$\frac{3}{4}$*yd (.7m) of $\frac{3}{4}$in (2cm) wide eyelet*
insertion lace
$\frac{3}{4}$*yd (.7m) of $\frac{3}{8}$in (1cm) wide green*
velvet ribbon

1 Cut out two 16in (40cm) squares from the green print fabric. Press 1in (2.5cm) hems to the wrong side all around each piece. Put aside one piece for the back.
2 Press $\frac{5}{8}$in (1.5cm) hems to the wrong side on each edge of the white eyelet fabric square. Pin the square in the center of the front section, on the right side. Baste $\frac{3}{8}$in (1cm) from folded edge.

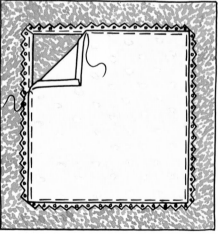

3 Lay the raw edge of the pointed edging under the fold of the eyelet lace fabric square. The edge of the square should overlap the edging by $\frac{1}{4}$in (5mm). Make tucks at the corners for a neat finish. Baste, then machine stitch through both layers.

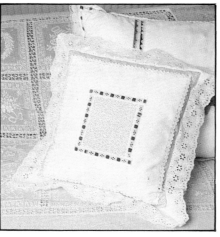

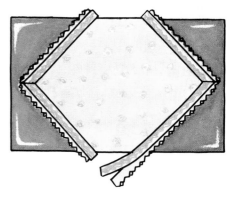

4 Cut out a 6in (16cm) square from the remaining green print fabric. Press $\frac{5}{8}$in (1.5cm) hems to the wrong side all around. Place this square in the center of the front section and baste in place. Thread the insertion lace with green velvet ribbon and cut the lace into four equal lengths. Baste a length of the lace over each side of the square to cover the edges, turning under the raw ends of the lace. Hand-sew along both edges, securing both the lace and the green printed fabric.

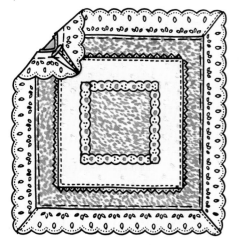

5 Baste the wide eyelet lace edging under the edge of the front section as shown, matching the raw edges of the lace to those on the fabric square. Make tucks at the corners by folding the excess fabric into a "V" shape on the wrong side of the eyelet lace edging, as shown in the drawing above.
Topstitch the tucks in place.
6 Pin, baste and then topstitch the front and back sections together, with wrong sides facing, stitching close to the edge and leaving one side open. Topstitch the eyelet lace edging to the front section along the open side, leaving the back edge free so that you can insert the pillow form.
Finally, slip the pillow form into the cover and sew up the opening neatly and invisibly by hand.

Small rectangular pillow

Size
12×16in (30×40cm).

Materials
White pillow form 12 × 16in (30 × 40cm)
$\frac{3}{8}$yd (.4m) of 36in (90cm) wide pale green satin or lightweight taffeta
$1\frac{3}{4}$yd (1.6m) of $1\frac{1}{2}$in (4cm) wide gathered eyelet lace edging
$1\frac{3}{4}$yd (1.6m) of $\frac{5}{8}$in (1.5cm) wide gathered eyelet lace edging
$12\frac{1}{2}$in (32cm) sq. eyelet lace fabric
$1\frac{1}{8}$yd (1m) of $\frac{3}{8}$in (1cm) wide green and pink braid
$1\frac{1}{8}$yd (1m) of $\frac{3}{8}$in (1cm) wide white lace edging
$\frac{3}{8}$yd (.3m) of narrow white ribbon

1 Cut out two rectangles $13\frac{1}{2} × 17\frac{1}{2}$in (34×44cm) from the green satin. Press $\frac{3}{4}$in (2cm) hems to the wrong side all around. Put one piece aside for the back.

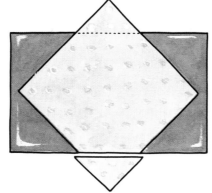

2 Press under $\frac{3}{8}$in (1cm) all around the square of eyelet lace fabric.
Pin the eyelet lace square diagonally to the green satin rectangle, making sure that it is properly centered, and trim away the corners of the eyelet lace at top and bottom, in line with the raw edges of the satin.
Neatly topstitch the eyelet lace fabric in place around all four sides close to the edge.

3 Cut the white lace edging into four equal lengths and stitch one piece along each diagonal edge of the eyelet lace fabric. Hand-sew a strip of green and pink braid over the edges of the edging and eyelet lace fabric.
4 Tie the white ribbon into a bow and sew it to the center of the front section of the eyelet lace fabric.

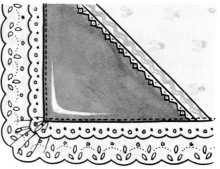

Terry Evans

5 Lay the narrower eyelet lace trim on top of the wider eyelet lace, with raw edges together. Stitch the two pieces together close to the raw edges. Baste eyelet lace trim to the turned-under edge of the front section with the narrower edging on top, extending $\frac{3}{8}$in (1cm) beyond the folded edge of the fabric.
6 Pin, baste and topstitch the front and back sections together close to the edge, leaving one end open for inserting the pillow form.
Topstitch the eyelet lace to the front section across the opening. Insert the pillow and sew up the opening invisibly by hand.

Homemaker

Baby go-round

Here is the lightweight answer to the problem of carrying a new baby around—a cozy portable bed with a firm base and two sturdy handles. It's perfect for infants up to about five months, when life is much easier if you can take your sleeping baby with you.

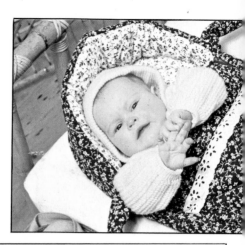

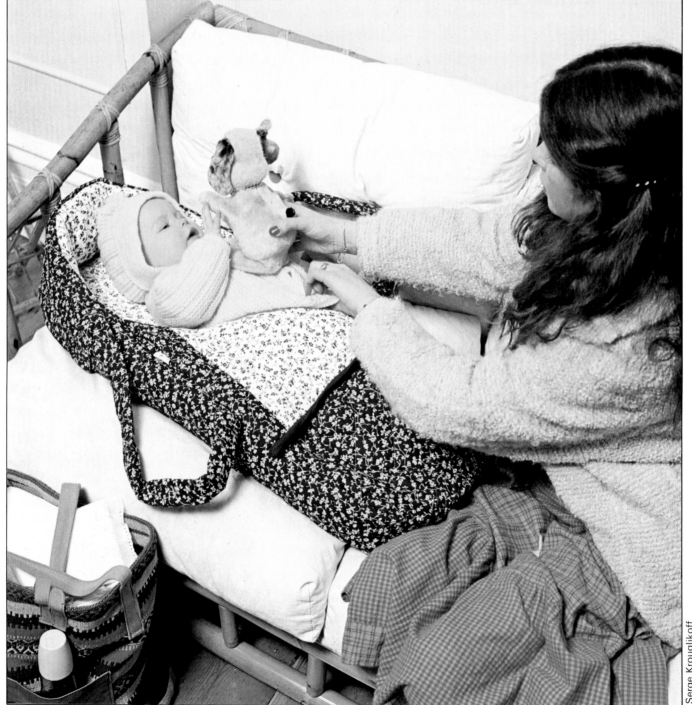

Measurements

The finished bed is $29\frac{1}{2}$in (75cm) long and 12in (30cm) wide. $\frac{5}{8}$in (1.5cm) seams are allowed throughout.

Materials

Piece of $\frac{1}{4}$in (5mm) thick particleboard
     $29\frac{1}{2} \times 12$in (75×30cm)
Coping saw
Sandpaper in various grades
Piece of $\frac{3}{8}$in (1cm) thick foam,
     $29\frac{1}{2} \times 12$in (75×30cm)
$2\frac{1}{4}$yd (2m) of 48in (122cm) wide
     reversible printed quilted cotton
$\frac{7}{8}$yd (.8m) of 48in (122cm) wide
     coordinated printed cotton fabric
$1\frac{1}{8}$yd (1m) of 37in (94cm) wide
     heavyweight polyester batting
18in (45cm) metal, heavy duty zipper
$\frac{1}{2}$yd (.4m) of 2in (5cm) wide white
     eyelet lace edging
$\frac{5}{8}$yd (.5m) of 1in (2.5cm) wide
     matching bias binding
Matching thread
Paper for pattern

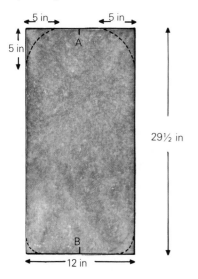

1 Round off the corners of the particleboard to give the desired shape of the bed, as shown. At the top end, mark two points 5in (12.5cm) from each corner. Similarly, mark off 5in (12.5cm) down each side. Draw a curved line joining the two points on each side.

Using a coping saw, cut away the corners along the curved lines. Sand the edges and, at the base end, sandpaper the corners.
2 Using the particleboard as your pattern, draw, then cut out the following pieces: one piece of foam, the same size as the board for the mattress; two pieces of printed fabric, $1\frac{1}{4}$in (3cm) larger than the board on the top and side edges and 4in (10cm) longer at the base, for the mattress cover; one piece of quilted fabric, $1\frac{1}{4}$in (3cm) larger than the board all around, for the base; one piece of quilted fabric, $\frac{5}{8}$in (1.5cm) larger than the board all around, for the top cover.

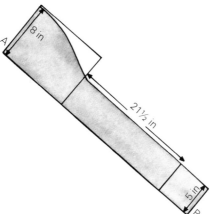

3 To make the pattern for the sides, measure the distance from A to B, as shown, on your quilted base fabric and add $1\frac{1}{4}$in (3cm) to this figure for seam allowance. From paper cut out a strip this length and 8in (20cm) wide. Shape this pattern as shown, so that base and sides are 5in (13cm) deep and the top slopes up to 8in (20cm) to form the head of the bed. Check that the pattern fits and add seam allowances.
4 Using this pattern, cut out four side pieces in quilted fabric and two side pieces in batting.
5 For the handles, cut out two strips of quilted fabric, each 43×6in (110×15cm).

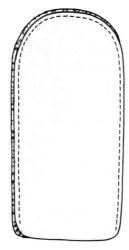

6 Place the two mattress cover pieces with right sides together; pin, baste and stitch around top and side edges.

7 Make a small double hem around the raw edges at the foot of the mattress cover to finish; pin, baste and topstitch.

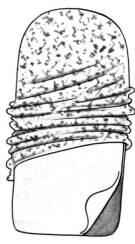

8 Place foam on one side of the board. Slip the mattress cover over the board and foam, tucking in the excess length of cover at the base, to envelop the board and hold the foam in place. Both the cover and the foam can easily be removed for washing.

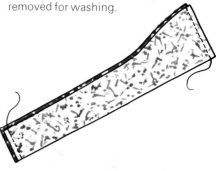

9 Place two quilted side pieces together with the dark sides facing. Pin, baste and stitch the short seams (A and B). This makes the outer side of the bed.

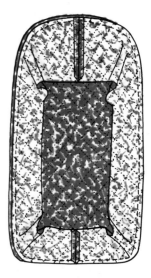

10 Pin, baste and stitch this outer side to the base, dark sides together, around the entire edge, matching seams A and B to the respective points on the base.

Terry Evans

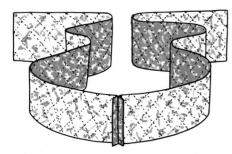

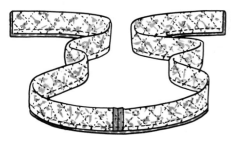

11 Pin, baste and stitch the two handle strips together along the short edges with dark sides facing, to form one long strip.

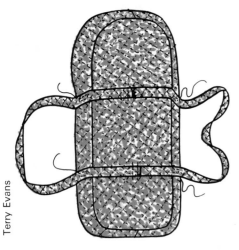

12 Fold handle in half lengthwise (dark side inside); pin, baste and stitch down long edge. Turn handle right side out. Turn in ends and slipstitch to finish. Place one end on top of the other and zig-zag stitch twice to form a good strong seam.

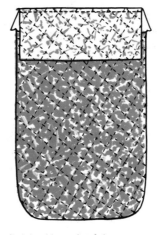

15 The finished length of the top cover must be 21½in (55cm). Turn back 10½in (27cm) along the upper edge of the cover. Insert the eyelet lace between the two layers, wrong side of edging downward, with the raw edge well into the fold. Pin, baste and stitch, ¼in (5mm) from folded edge. Turn top cover back flat.
16 Fold under the raw edge of the cover, 3in (8cm) above the eyelet lace. (Check that top cover measures 21½in [55cm] in length, plus seam allowance.) Baste along the folded edge. Trim the hem allowance to 2in (5cm). Turn under ⅜in (1cm) and hem in place.

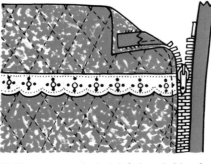

17 Pin, baste and stitch left-hand side of the zipper to the right-hand side of the top cover so that the zipper teeth are ¼in (5mm) from the top. Turn under the top of zipper tape and hand sew it in place.
18 Fold bias binding in half, lengthwise, enclosing raw edges of seam allowance and zipper, turning in upper raw edge of binding. Hand sew in place along upper end and down each side. Cut off excess tape at lower end, leaving ¾in (2cm).

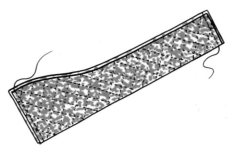

19 Pin, baste and stitch the remaining two side pieces together, with light sides

facing, at the short edges "A" and "B."
20 Pin, baste and stitch the batting side pieces together at short edges.
21 With dark (right) sides together pin and baste the top cover to the outer side piece (already attached) matching edges and starting with the left-hand side of the cover (opposite the zipper) and working around to the base of the zipper. With the zipper closed, continue pinning and basting the zipper to the right-hand side.
22 Pin and baste the light sides to the top edge of the already-attached side pieces, with right sides together, matching raw edges. The seam allowance of the top cover will be sandwiched between the two side layers.
23 Finally, pin and baste the batting sides in place on top of the fabric sides, matching top edges.

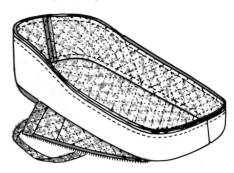

24 Stitch all around, through all three layers of sides and top cover, catching in right-hand side of zipper.
25 Turn under raw edge of bias binding at base of zipper and carefully hand sew in place to finish.
26 Turn the sides of the bed right side out so that batting is now enclosed between the two fabric layers. Trim off seam allowance of batting along inside edge. Turn under raw edge of inner side piece and hand sew in place.
27 Fit mattress inside the bed with foam side up.

13 Pin and baste handle in place, on base and sides, as shown. When held by the handles the empty bed should slope gently downward at the foot (to compensate for the weight of the baby's head). If possible, carefully test the balance with the baby in the bed and, if necessary, reposition the handles so that bed with baby will be horizontal in use.
14 Stitch the handles in place securely at sides and on underside of base, using a double row of stitching at base and side positions, as shown, to make the handles as strong as possible.
Note: It is essential that all work on the handles be done with great care, as they must carry the weight of the baby when the bed is in use.

Terry Evans